FLORENCE NIGHTINGALE
TO HER NURSES

MACMILLAN AND CO., Limited
LONDON · BOMBAY · CALCUTTA
MELBOURNE

THE MACMILLAN COMPANY
NEW YORK · BOSTON · CHICAGO
DALLAS · SAN FRANCISCO

THE MACMILLAN CO. OF CANADA, Ltd.
TORONTO

Florence Nightingale

Florence Nightingale to her Nurses

A SELECTION FROM MISS NIGHTINGALE'S
ADDRESSES TO PROBATIONERS AND NURSES
OF THE NIGHTINGALE SCHOOL AT
ST. THOMAS'S HOSPITAL

MACMILLAN AND CO., LIMITED
ST. MARTIN'S STREET, LONDON
1915

PREFACE

Between 1872 and 1900 Miss Nightingale used, when she was able, to send an annual letter or address to the probationer-nurses of the Nightingale School at St. Thomas' Hospital, "and the nurses who have been trained there."[1] These addresses were usually read aloud by Sir Harry Verney, the chairman of the Nightingale Fund, in the presence of the probationers and nurses, and a printed copy or a lithographed facsimile of the manuscript was given to each of the nurses present, "for private use only." A few also were written for the Nightingale Nurses serving in Edinburgh.

The letters were not meant for publication, and indeed are hardly suitable to be printed as a whole

---

[1] The beginning of the first address will suggest a reason for this turn of phrase. A nurse who had been through training might not always be "worthy of the name of 'Trained Nurse'" (Address of 1876).

as there is naturally a good deal of repetition in them. Since Miss Nightingale's death, however, heads of nursing institutions and others have asked for copies of the addresses to be read or given to nurses, and her family hope that the publication of a selection may do something to carry further the intention with which they were originally written.

Perhaps, too, not only nurses, but others, may care to read some of these letters. There is a natural desire to understand the nature of a great man's or woman's influence, and we see in the addresses something at least of what constituted Miss Nightingale's power. Her earnest care for the nurses, her intense desire that they should be " perfect," speak in every line. They do not, of course, give full expression to the writer's mind. They were written after she had reached middle age, as from a teacher of long and wide experience to pupils much younger than herself—pupils some of whom had had very little schooling and did not easily read or write. The want of even elementary education and of habits and traditions of discipline which grow in schools are difficulties less felt now than in 1872, when Miss Nightingale's first letter to nurses was written. At that time it was necessary in addressing such an audience to write very simply, without learned allusions (though some such appear in disguise) and without too great severity and concentration of style. The familiar words of the Bible and hymns could appeal to the least learned among her hearers, and never lost their power with Miss Nightingale herself.

But through the simple and popular style of the addresses something of a philosophical framework can be seen. When Miss Nightingale hopes that her nurses are a step further on the way to becoming " perfect as our Father in Heaven is perfect," she has in mind the conception she had formed of a moral government of the world in which science, activity, and religion were one. In her unpublished writings these ideas are dwelt on again and again. They are clearly explained in her note on a prayer of St. Teresa :—

" We cannot really attach any meaning to *perfect* thought and feeling, unless its perfection has been attained through life and work, unless it is being realised in life and work. It is in fact a contradiction to suppose Perfection to exist except at work, to exist without exercise, without 'working out.' We cannot conceive of *perfect* wisdom, perfect happiness, except as having *attained*, attained perfection through work. The ideas of the Impassible and of Perfection are contradictions. . . . This seems to be the very meaning of the word 'perfect'—'made through'—made perfect through suffering—completed—working out ; and even the only idea we can form of the *Perfect Perfect* . . . 'God in us,' 'grieving the Holy Spirit of God,' 'My Father worketh and I work'—these seem all indications of this truth. . . . We cannot explain or conceive of Perfection except as having worked through Imperfection or sin. . . . The Eternal Perfect almost pre-supposes the Eternal Imperfect." Hence her deep interest in the "laws which register the connection of physical conditions with moral actions." She quotes elsewhere a scientific writer who delighted in the consciousness that his books were to the best of his ability expounding the ways of God to man. "I can truly say," she continues, "that the feeling he describes has been ever present to my mind. Whether in having a drain cleaned out, or in ventilating a hospital ward, or in urging the principles of healthy construction of buildings, or of temperance and useful occupation, or of sewerage and water supply, I always considered myself as obeying a direct command of God, and it was ' with the earnestness and reverence due to ' God's laws that I urged them. . . . For mankind to create the circumstances which create mankind through these His Laws is the ' way of God.' "

The letters have needed a little editing. Miss Nightingale had great power of succinct and forcible statement on occasion, but here she was not tabulating statistics nor making a businesslike summary for a Minister in a hurry. Certain ideas had to be impressed, in the first place orally, on minds which were not all highly trained ; and for this she naturally wrote in a discursive way. She did not correct the proofs. As readers of her *Life* will know, she was burdened with other work and delicate health, and she found any considerable revision difficult and uncongenial. It has therefore been necessary to make a few emendations, such as occasionally correcting an obvious misprint, adding a missing word, and taking out brackets, stops, and divisions which obscured the sense. A few of the many repetitions and one or two passages only interesting at the time, have also been left out. The object has been to change as little as possible, and I hope nothing has been done that Miss Nightingale would not have done herself if she had corrected the proofs. The first two addresses give perhaps the fullest expression of the main theme to which she returns again and again. Others have been chosen chiefly for the sake of characteristic illustrations of the same theme.

ROSALIND NASH.

I

FOR us who Nurse, our Nursing is a thing, which, unless in it we are making *progress* every year, every month, every week, take my word for it we are going *back*.

The more experience we gain, the more progress we can make. The progress you make in your year's training with us is as nothing to what you must make every year *after* your year's training is over.

A woman who thinks in herself: "Now I am a 'full' Nurse, a 'skilled' Nurse, I have learnt all that there is to be learnt": take my word for it, she does not know *what a Nurse is*, and she never *will* know; she is *gone* back already.

Conceit and Nursing cannot exist in the same person, any more than new patches on an old garment.

B

Every year of her service a good Nurse will say : " I learn something every day."

I have had more experience in all countries and in different ways of Hospitals than almost any one ever had before (there were no opportunities for learning in *my* youth such as you have had) ; but if I could recover strength so much as to walk about, I would begin all over again. I would come for a year's training to St. Thomas' Hospital under your admirable Matron (and I venture to add that she would find me the closest in obedience to all our rules), sure that I should learn every day, learn all the more for my past experience.

And then I would try to be learning every day to the last hour of my life. " And when his legs were cuttit off, He fought upon his stumps," says the ballad ; so, when I could no longer learn by nursing others, I would learn by being nursed, by seeing Nurses practise upon *me*. It is all experience.

Agnes Jones, who died as Matron of the Liverpool Workhouse Infirmary (whom you may have heard of as " Una "), wrote from the Workhouse in the last year of her life : " I mean to stay at this post forty years, God willing ; but I must come back to St. Thomas' as soon as I

have a holiday ; I shall learn so much more"
(she had been a year at St. Thomas') "now that
I have more experience."

When I was a child, I remember reading that
Sir Isaac Newton, who was, as you know, perhaps
the greatest discoverer among the Stars and the
Earth's wonders who ever lived, said in his last
hours : "I seem to myself like a child who has
been playing with a few pebbles on the sea-shore,
leaving unsearched all the wonders of the great
Ocean beyond."

By the side of this put a Nurse leaving her
Training School and reckoning up what she has
learnt, ending with—"The only wonder is that
one head can contain it all." (What a small head
it must be then !)

I seem to have remembered all through life Sir
Isaac Newton's words.

And to nurse—that is, under Doctor's orders,
to cure or to prevent sickness and maiming, Surgical and Medical,—is a field, a road, of which one
may safely say : There is no end—no end in what
we may be learning every day.[1]

---

[1] There is a well-known Society abroad (for charitable works) of which
the Members go through a two years' probation on their first entering, but
after ten years they return and go through a second probation of one year.
This is one of the most striking recognitions I know of the fact that

I have sometimes heard : " But have we not reason to be conceited, when we compare ourselves to . . . and . . . ? " (naming drinking, immoral, careless, dishonest Nurses). I will not think it possible that such things can ever be said among *us*. Taking it even upon the worldly ground, what woman among us, instead of looking to that which is higher, will of her own accord compare herself with that which is lower—with immoral women ?

Does not the Apostle say : " I count not myself to have apprehended : but this one thing I do, forgetting those things which are behind, *and reaching forth unto those things which are before, I press toward* the mark for the prize of the *high calling* of God in Christ Jesus " ; and what higher " calling " can we have than Nursing ? But then we must " press forward " ; we have indeed *not* " apprehended " if we have not " apprehended " even so much as this.

There is a little story about " the Pharisee " known over all Christendom. Should Christ come again upon the earth, would He have to apply that parable to us ?

---

progress is always to be made : that grown-up people, even of middle-age, ought always to have their education going on. But only those *can* learn *after* middle age who have gone on learning up to middle age.

And now, let me say a thing which I am sure must have been in all your minds before this : if, unless we improve every day in our Nursing, we are going back : how much more must it be, that, unless we improve every day in our conduct as Christian women, followers of Him by whose name we call ourselves, we shall be going back ?

This applies of course to every woman in the world ; but it applies more especially to us, because we know no one calling in the world, except it be that of teaching, in which *what we can do* depends so much upon *what we are*. To be *a good Nurse* one must be *a good woman* ; or one is truly nothing but a tinkling bell. To be a good woman at all, one must be an improving woman ; for stagnant waters sooner or later, and stagnant air, as we know ourselves, always grow corrupt and unfit for use.

Is any one of us a *stagnant woman*? Let it not have to be said by any one of us : I left this Home a worse woman than I came into it. I came in with earnest purpose, and now I think of little but my own satisfaction and a good place.

When the head and the hands are very full, as in Nursing, it is so easy, so very easy, if the heart has not an earnest purpose for God and our neighbour, to end in doing one's work only for oneself, and not at all—even when we seem to be serving our neighbours—not at all for them or for God.

I should hardly like to talk of a subject which, after all, must be very much between each one of us and her God,—which is hardly a matter for *talk* at all, and certainly not for me, who cannot be among you (though there is nothing in the world I should so dearly wish), but that I thought perhaps you might like to hear of things which persons in the same situation, that is, in different Training Schools on the Continent, have said to me.

I will mention two or three :

1. One said, " The greatest help I ever had in life was that we were taught in our Training School always to raise our hearts to God the first thing on waking in the morning."

Now it need hardly be said that we cannot make a rule for this ; a rule will not teach this, any more than making a rule that the chimney shall not smoke will make the smoke go up the chimney.

If we occupy ourselves the last thing at night

with rushing about, gossiping in one another's rooms; if our last thoughts at night are of some slight against ourselves, or spite against another, or about each other's tempers, it is needless to say that our first thoughts in the morning will not be of God.

Perhaps there may even have been some quarrel; and if those who pretend to be educated women indulge in these irreligious uneducated disputes, what a scandal before those less educated, to whom an example, not a stone of offence, should be set!

"A thousand irreligious cursed hours" (as some poet says), have not seldom, in the lives of all but a few whom we may truly call Saints upon earth, been spent on some feeling of ill-will. And can we expect to be really able to lift up our hearts the first thing in the morning to the God of "good will towards men" if we do this?

I speak for myself, even more perhaps than for others.

2. Another woman [1] once said to me :—"I was taught in my Training School never to have those long inward discussions with myself, those inter-

---

[1] The Madre Santa Colomba, of the Convent of the Trinità dei Monti in Rome.—EDITOR'S NOTE.

minable conversations inside myself, which make up so much more of our own thoughts than we are aware. If it was something about my duties, I went straight to my Superiors, and asked for leave or advice ; if it was any of those useless or ill-tempered thoughts about one another, or those that were put over us, we were taught to lay them before God and get the better of them, before they got the better of us."

A spark can be put out while it is a spark, if it falls on our dress, but not when it has set the whole dress in flames. So it is with an ill-tempered thought against another. And who will tell how much of our thoughts these occupy ?

I suppose, of course, that those who think themselves better than others are bent upon setting them a better example.

II

And this brings me to something else. (I can always correct others though I cannot always correct myself.) It is about jealousies and punctilios as to ranks, classes, and offices, when employed in one good work. What an injury this jealous woman is doing, not to others, or not to others so much as to herself ; she is doing it to herself ! She is not getting out of her work the advantage, the improvement to her own character, the nobleness (for to be useful is the only true nobleness) which God has appointed her that work to attain. She is not getting out of her work what God has given it her for ; but just the contrary.

(Nurses are not children, but women ; and if they can't do this for themselves, no one can for them.)

I think it is one of Shakespeare's heroes who says " I laboured to be wretched." How true that is ! How true it is of some people all their lives ; and perhaps there is not one of us who could not say it with truth of herself at one time or other : I laboured to be mean and contemptible and small and ill-tempered, by being revengeful of petty slights.

A woman once said : " What signifies it to me that this one does me an injury or the other speaks ill of me, if I do not deserve it ? The injury strikes God before it strikes me, and if He forgives it, why should not I ? I hope I love Him better than I do myself." This may sound fanciful ; but is there not truth in it ?

What a privilege it is, the work that God has given us Nurses to do, if we will only let Him have

His own way with us—a greater privilege to my mind than He has given to any woman (except to those who are teachers), because *we* can always be useful, always "ministering" to others, real followers of Him who said that He came "not to be ministered unto" but to minister. Cannot we fancy Him saying to *us*, If any one thinks herself greater among you, let her minister unto others.

This is not to say that we are to be doing other people's work. Quite the reverse. The very essence of all good organisation is that everybody should do her (or his) own work in such a way as to help and not to hinder every one else's work.

But this being arranged, that any one should say, I am "put upon" by having to associate with so-and-so ; or by *not* having so-and-so to associate with ; or, by not having such a post ; or, by having such a post ; or, by my Superiors "walking upon me," or, "dancing" upon me (you may laugh, but such things have actually been said), or etc., etc.,— this is simply making the peace of God impossible, the call of God (for in all work He calls us) of none effect ; it is grieving the Spirit of God ; it is doing our best to make all free-will associations intolerable.

In "Religious Orders" this is provided against

by enforcing blind, unconditional obedience through the fears and promises of a Church.

Does it not seem to you that the greater freedom of secular Nursing Institutions, as it requires (or ought to require) greater individual responsibility, greater self-command in each one, greater nobleness in each, greater *self-possession* in *patience*—so, that very need of self-possession, of greater nobleness in each, requires (or ought to require) greater thought in each, more discretion, and higher, not less, obedience ? For the obedience of intelligence, not the obedience of slavery, is what *we* want.

The slave obeys with stupid obedience, with deceitful evasion of service, or with careless eye service. Now, we cannot suppose God to be satisfied or pleased with stupidity and carelessness. The free woman in Christ obeys, or rather *seconds* all the rules, all the orders given her, with intelligence, with all her heart, and with all her strength, and with all her *mind*.

"Not slothful in business; fervent in spirit, serving the Lord."

And you who have to be Head Nurses, or Sisters of Wards, well know what I mean, for you have to be Ward *Mistresses* as well as Nurses; and how can she (the Ward Mistress) command if she has not learnt how to obey ? If she cannot enforce upon herself to obey rules with discretion, how can she enforce upon her Ward to obey rules with discretion ?

III

And of those who have to be Ward Mistresses, as well as those who are Ward Mistresses already, or in any charge of trust or authority, I will ask, if Sisters and Head Nurses will allow me to ask of them, as I have so often asked of myself—

What is it that made our Lord speak "as one having authority " ? What was the key to *His* "authority " ? Is it anything which we, trying to be " like Him," could have—like Him ?

What are the qualities which give us authority, which enable us to exercise some charge or control over others with "authority "? It is not the charge or position itself, for we often see persons in a position of authority, who have no authority at all ; and on the other hand we sometimes see persons in the very humblest position who exercise a great influence or authority on all around them.

The very first element for having control over others is, of course, to have control over oneself. If I cannot take charge of myself, I cannot take charge of others. The next, perhaps, is—not to try to "seem" anything, but to *be* what we would *seem*.

A person in charge must be felt more than she is heard—not heard more than she is felt. She must fulfil her charge without noisy disputes, by the silent power of a consistent life, in which there is no *seeming*, and no hiding, but plenty of discretion. She must exercise authority without appearing to exercise it.

A person, but more especially a woman, in charge must have a quieter and more impartial mind than those under her, in order to influence them by the best part of them and not by the worst.

We (Sisters) think that we must often make allowances for them, and sometimes put ourselves in their place. And I will appeal to Sisters to say whether we must not observe more than we speak, instead of speaking more than we observe. We must not give an order, much less a reproof, without being fully acquainted with both sides of the case. Else, having scolded wrongfully, we look rather foolish.

The person in charge every one must see to be just and candid, looking at both sides, not moved by entreaties or, by likes and dislikes, but only by justice ; and always reasonable, remembering and not forgetting the wants of those of whom she is in charge.

She must have a keen though generous insight into the characters of those she has to control. They must know that she *cares for* them even while she is checking them ; or rather that she checks them *because* she cares for them. A woman *thus* reproved is often made your friend for life ; a word dropped in this way by a Sister in charge (I am speaking now solely to Sisters and Head Nurses) may sometimes show a probationer the unspeakable importance of this year of her life, when she must sow the seed of her future nursing in this world, and of her future life through eternity. For although future years are of importance to train the plant and make it come up, yet if there is no seed nothing will come up.

Nay, I appeal again to Sisters' own experience, whether they have not known patients feel the same of words dropped before *them*.

We had in one of the Hospitals which we nurse a little girl patient of seven years old, the child of a bad mother, who used to pray on her

knees (when she did not know she was heard)
her own little prayer that she might not forget,
when she went away to what she already knew to
be a bad life, the good words she had been taught.
(In this great London, the time that children
spend in Hospital is sometimes the only time in
their lives that they hear good words.) And
sometimes we have had patients, widows or
journeymen for instance, who had striven to the
last to do for their children and place them all out
in service or at work, die in our Hospitals, thank-
ing God that they had had this time to collect
their thoughts before death, and to die " so
comfortably " as they expressed it.

But, if a Ward is not kept in such a spirit that
patients can collect their thoughts, whether it is
for life or for death, and that children can hear
good words, of course these things will not happen.

Ward management is only made possible by
kindness and sympathy. And the mere way in
which a thing is said or done to patient, or probationer, makes all the difference. In a Ward,
too, where there is no *order* there can be no
" authority " ; there must be noise and dispute.

Hospital Sisters are the only women who may
be in charge really of men. Is this not enough

to show how essential to them are those qualities which alone constitute real authority ?

Never to have a quarrel with another ; never to say things which rankle in another's mind ; never when we are uncomfortable ourselves to make others uncomfortable—for quarrels come out of such very small matters, a hasty word, a sharp joke, a harsh order : without regard to these things, how can we take charge ?

We may say, so-and-so is too weak if she minds that. But, pray, are we not weak in the same way ourselves ?

I have been in positions of authority myself and have always tried to remember that to use such an advantage inconsiderately is—cowardly. To be sharp upon them is worse in me than in them to be sharp upon me. No one can trample upon others, and govern them. To win them is half, I might say the whole, secret of " having charge." If you find your way to their hearts, you may do what you like with them ; and that authority is the most complete which is least perceived or asserted.

The world, whether of a Ward or of an Empire, is governed not by many words but by few ; though some, especially women, seem to

expect to govern by many words—by talk, and
nothing else.

There is scarcely anything which interferes so
much with charge over others as rash and in-
considerate talking, or as wearing one's thoughts
on one's cap. There is scarcely anything which
interferes so much with their respect for us as any
want of simplicity in us. A person who is
always thinking of herself—how she looks, what
effect she produces upon others, what others will
think or say of her—can scarcely ever hope to
have charge of them to any purpose.

We ought to be what we want to seem, or
those under us will find out very soon that we
only seem what we ought to be.

If we think only of the duty we have in hand,
we may hope to make the others think of it too.
But if we are fidgety or uneasy about trifles, can
we hope to impress them with the importance of
essential things?

There is so much talk about persons now-a-
days. Everybody criticises everybody. Everybody
seems liable to be drawn into a current, against
somebody, or in favour of every one doing what
she likes, pleasing herself, or getting promotion.

If any one gives way to all these distractions,

and has no root of calmness in herself, she will not find it in any Hospital or Home.

"All this is as old as the hills," you will say. Yes, it is as old as Christianity; and is not that the more reason for us to begin to practise it to-day?   "*To-day*, if ye will hear my voice," says the Father; "*To-day* ye shall be with me in Paradise," says the Son; and He does not say this only to the dying; for Heaven may begin here, and "The kingdom of heaven is within," He tells us.

Most of you here present will be in a few years in charge of others, filling posts of responsibility. *All* are on the threshold of active life.   Then our characters will be put to the test, whether in some position of charge or of subordination, or both. Shall we be found wanting?   Unable to control ourselves, therefore unable to control others? With many good qualities, perhaps, but owing to selfishness, conceit, to some want of purpose, some laxness, carelessness, lightness, vanity, some temper, habits of self-indulgence, or want of disinterested-ness, unequal to the struggle of life, the business of life, and ill-adapted to the employment of Nursing, which we have chosen for ourselves, and which, almost above all others, requires earnest

purpose, and the reverse of all these faults?
Thirty years hence, if we could suppose us all
standing here again passing judgment on ourselves,
and telling sincerely why one has succeeded and
another has failed ; why the life of one has been
a blessing to those she has charge of, and another
has gone from one thing to another, pleasing
herself, and bringing nothing to good — what
would we give to be able *now* to see all this
before us ?

Yet some of those reasons for failure or success
we may anticipate now. Because so-and-so was or
was not weak or vain ; because she could or could
not make herself respected ; because she had no
steadfastness in her, or on the contrary because
she had a fixed and steady purpose ; because
she was selfish or unselfish, disliked or beloved ;
because she could or could not keep her women
together or manage her patients, or was or was
not to be trusted in Ward business. And there
are many other reasons which I might give you,
or which you might give yourselves, for the success
or failure of those who have passed through this
Training School for the last eleven years.

Can we not see ourselves as others see us ?

For the " world is a hard schoolmaster," and

punishes us without giving reasons, and much more severely than any Training School can, and when we can no longer perhaps correct the defect.

Good posts may be found for us ; but can we keep them so as to fill them worthily ? Or are we but unprofitable servants in fulfilling any charge?

Yet many of us are blinded to the truth by our own self-love even to the end. And we attribute to accident or ill-luck what is really the consequence of some weakness or error in ourselves.

But " can we not see ourselves as God sees us ? " is a still more important question. For while we value the judgments of our superiors, and of our fellows, which may correct our own judgments, we must also have a higher standard which may correct theirs. We cannot altogether trust them, and still less can we trust ourselves. And we know, of course, that the worth of a life is not altogether measured by failure or success. We want to see our purposes, and the ways we take to fulfil such charge as may be given us, as they are in the sight of God. " Thou God seest me."

And thus do we return to the question we asked before—how near can we come to Him whose name we bear, when we call ourselves Christians ? How

near to His gentleness and goodness—to His
"authority" over others.[1]

And the highest "authority" which a woman
especially can attain among her fellow women must
come from her doing God's work here in the same
spirit, and with the same thoroughness, that Christ
did, though we follow him but "afar off."

IV

Lastly, it is charity to nurse sick bodies well;
it is greater charity to nurse well and patiently sick
minds, tiresome sufferers. But there is a greater
charity even than these : to do good to those who
are not good to us, to behave well to those who
behave ill to us, to serve with love those who do
not even receive our service with good temper, to
forgive on the instant any slight which we may
have received, or may have fancied we have received,
or any worse injury.

[1] There is a most suggestive story told of one, some 300 years ago, an
able and learned man, who presented himself for admission into a Society
for Preaching and Charitable Works. He was kept for many months on
this query : *Are you a Christian?* by his "Master of Probationers." He
took kindly and heartily to it ; went with his whole soul and mind into this
little momentous question, and solved it victoriously in his own course, and
in his after course of usefulness for others. Am I a Christian? is most
certainly the first and most important question for each one of us Nurses.
Let us ask it, each of herself, every day.

If we cannot "do good" to those who "persecute" us—for we are not "persecuted": if we cannot pray "Father, forgive them, for they know not what they do"—for none are nailing us to a cross : how much more must we try to serve with patience and love any who use us spitefully, to nurse with all our hearts any thankless peevish patients !

We Nurses may well call ourselves "blessed among women" in this, that we can be always exercising all these three charities, and so fulfil the work our God has given us to do.

Just as I was writing this came a letter from Mrs. Beecher Stowe, who wrote *Uncle Tom's Cabin.* She has so fallen in love with the character of our Agnes Jones ("Una")[1] which she had just read, that she asks about the progress of our work, supposing that we have many more Unas. They wish to "organise a similar movement" in America —a "movement" of Unas—what a great thing that would be ! Shall we all try to be Unas?

She ends, as I wish to end,—"Yours, in the dear name that is above every other,"

FLORENCE NIGHTINGALE.

[1] Nightingale Nurse and Lady Superintendent of Liverpool Workhouse Infirmary. Pioneer of Workhouse Nursing. After her early death in 1868 Miss Nightingale wrote in *Good Words* an article, "Una and the Lion," on her life and work.—EDITOR'S NOTE.

II

May 23, 1873.

My dear Friends,—Another year has passed over us. Nearly though not quite all of us who were here at this time last year have gone their several ways, to their several posts; some at St. Thomas', some to Edinburgh, some to Highgate. Nearly all are, I am thankful to say, well, and I hope we may say happy. Some are gone altogether.

May this year have set us all one step farther, one year on our way to becoming "perfect as our Father in Heaven is perfect," as it ought to have done.

Some differences have been made in the School by our good Matron, who toils for us early and late—to bring us on the way, we hope, towards becoming "perfect."

These differences—I leave it to you to say, improvements—are as you see : our new Medical Instructor having vigorously taken us in hand and giving us his invaluable teaching (1) in Medical and Surgical Nursing, (2) in the elements of Anatomy. I need not say : Let us profit.

Next, in order to give more time and leisure to less tired bodies, the Special Probationers have two afternoons in the week off duty for the course of reading which our able Medical Instructor has laid down. And the Nurse-Probationers have all one morning and one afternoon in the week to improve themselves, in which our kind Home Sister assists them by classes. And, again, I need not say how important it is to take the utmost advantage of this. Do not let the world move on and leave us in the wrong. Now that, by the law of the land, every child between five and thirteen must be at school, it will be a poor tale, indeed, in their after life for Nurses who cannot read, write, spell, and cypher well and correctly, and read aloud easily, and take notes of the temperature of cases, and the like. Only this last week, I was told by one of our own Matrons of an excellent Nurse of her own to whom she would have given a good place, only that she could neither read nor write well enough for it.

And may I tell you, not for envy, but for a generous rivalry, that you will have to work hard if you wish St. Thomas' Training School to hold its own with other Schools rising up.

Let us be on our guard against the danger, not exactly of thinking too well of ourselves (for no one consciously does this), but of isolating ourselves, of falling into party spirit—always remembering that, if we can do any good to others, we must draw others to us by the influence of our characters, and not by any profession of what we are—least of all, by a profession of Religion.

And this, by the way, applies peculiarly to what we are with our patients. Least of all should a *woman* try to exercise religious influence with her patients, as it were, by a ministry, a chaplaincy. We are not chaplains. It is what she *is* in *herself*, and what comes out of herself, out of what she *is*— that exercise a moral or religious influence over her patients. No set form of words is of any use. And patients are so quick to see whether a Nurse is consistent always in herself—whether she *is* what she *says* to them. And if she is not, it is no use. *If she is*, of how much use, unawares to herself, may the simplest word of soothing, of comfort, or even of reproof—especially in the quiet night—be to the roughest patient, who is there from drink, or to the still innocent child, or to the anxious toil-worn mother or husband ! But if she wishes to do this, she must keep up a sort of divine calm and high sense of duty in her own mind. Christ was alone, from time to time, in the wilderness or on mountains. If *He* needed this, how much more must we ?

Quiet in our own rooms (and a room of your own is specially provided for each one here) ; a few minutes of calm thought to offer up the day to God : how indispensable it is, in this ever increasing hurry of life ! When we live " so fast," do we not require a breathing time, a moment or two daily, to think where we are going ? At this time, especially, when we are laying the foundation of our after life, in reality the most important time of all.

And I am not at all saying that our patients have everything to learn from *us*. On the contrary, we can, many a time, learn from them, in patience, in true religious feeling and hope. One of our Sisters told me that she had often learnt more from her patients than from any one else. And I am sure I can say the same for myself. The poorest, the meanest, the humblest patient may enter into the kingdom of Heaven before the cleverest of us, or the most conceited. For, in another world, many, many of the conditions of this world must be changed. Do we think of this?

We have been, almost all of us, taught to pray in the days of our childhood. Is there not something sad and strange in our throwing this aside when most required by us, on the threshold of our active lives? Life is a shallow thing, and more especially *Hospital* life, without any depth of religion. For it is a matter of simple experience that the best things, the things which seem as if they most would make us feel, become the most hardening if not rightly used.

And may I say a thing from my own experience? No training is of any use, unless one can learn (1) to feel, and (2) to think out things for oneself. And if we have not true religious feeling and purpose, Hospital life—the highest of all things *with* these—*without* them becomes a mere routine and bustle, and a very hardening routine and bustle.

One of our past Probationers said : " Our work must be the first thing, but God must be in it." " And He is not in it," she added. But let us hope that this is not so. I am sure it was not so with *her*. Let us try to make it not so with any of us.

There are three things which one must have to

prevent this degeneration in oneself. And let each one of us, from time to time, tell, not any one else, but herself, whether she has these less or more than when she began her training here.

One is the real, deep, religious feeling and strong, personal, motherly interest for each one of our patients. And you can see this motherly interest in girls of twenty-one—we have had Sisters of not more than that age who had it—and *not* see it in women of forty.

The second is a strong practical (intellectual, if you will) interest in the *case*, how it is going on. This is what makes the true Nurse. Otherwise the patients might as well be pieces of furniture, and we the housemaids, unless we see how interesting a thing Nursing is. This is what makes us urge you to begin to observe the very first case you see.

The third is the pleasures of administration, which, though a fine word, means only learning to manage a Ward well : to keep it fresh, clean, tidy ; to keep up its good order, punctuality ; to report your cases with absolute accuracy to the Surgeon or Physician, and first to report them to the Sister ; and to do all that is contained in the one word, Ward-management : to keep wine-lists, diet-lists, washing-lists——that is Sister's work——and to do all the things no less important which constitute Nurse's work.

But it would take a whole book for me to count up these ; and I am going back to the first thing that we were saying : without deep religious purpose how shallow a thing is Hospital life, which is, or ought to be, the most inspiring ! For, as years go on, we shall have others to train ; and find that the springs of religion are dried up within ourselves. The patients we shall always have with us while we are Nurses. And we shall find that we have no religious gift or influence with them, no word in season, whether for those who are to live, or for those who are to die, no, not even when they are in their last hours, and perhaps no one by but *us* to speak a word to point them to the Eternal Father and Saviour ; not even for a poor little dying child who cries : " Nursey, tell me, oh, why is it so dark ? " Then we may feel painfully about them what we do not at present feel about ourselves. We may wish, both for our patients and Probationers, that they had the restraints of the " fear " of the most Holy God, to enable them to resist the temptation. We may regret that our own Probationers seem so worldly and external. And we may perceive too late that the deficiency in their characters began in our own.

For, to all good women, *life* is a prayer ; and though we pray in our own rooms, in the Wards and at Church, the end must not be confounded with the means. We are the more bound to watch strictly over ourselves ; we have not less but more need of a high standard of duty and of life in our Nursing ; we must teach ourselves humility and modesty by becoming more aware of our own weakness and narrowness, and liability to mistake as Nurses and as Christians. Mere worldly success to any nobler, higher mind is not worth having. Do you think Agnes Jones, or some who are now living amongst us, cared much about worldly success? They cared about efficiency, thoroughness. But that is a different thing.

We must condemn many of our own tempers when we calmly review them. We must lament over training opportunities which we have lost, must desire to become better women, better Nurses. That we all of us must feel. And then, and not till then, will *life* and *work* among the sick become a prayer.

For prayer is communion or co-operation with God: the expression of a *life* among his poor and sick

and erring ones.   But when we speak with God, our
power of addressing Him, of holding communion
with Him, and listening to His still small voice,
depends upon our will being one and the same with
His.   *Is* He our God, as He was Christ's ?   To
Christ He was all, to us He seems sometimes
nothing.   Can we retire to rest after our busy,
anxious day in the Wards, with the feeling : "Lord,
into Thy hands I commend my spirit," and those
of such and such anxious cases ; remembering, too,
that in the darkness, " Thou God seest me," and
seest them too ?   Can we rise in the morning,
almost with a feeling of joy that we are spared
another day to do Him service with His sick ?—

> Awake, my soul, and with the sun,
> Thy daily stage of duty run.

Does the thought ever occur to us in the course
of the day, that we will correct that particular fault
of mind, or heart, or temper, whether slowness, or
bustle, or want of accuracy or method, or harsh
judgments, or want of loyalty to those under whom
or among whom we are placed, or sharp talking, or
tale-bearing or gossiping—oh, how common, and
how old a fault, as old as Solomon !   "He that
repeateth a matter, separateth friends ; " and how
can people trust us unless they know that we are

not tale-bearers, who will misrepresent or improperly repeat what is said to us? Shall we correct this, or any other fault, not with a view to our success in life, or to our own credit, but in order that we may be able to serve our Master better in the service of the sick? Or do we ever seek to carry on the battle against light behaviour, against self-indulgence, against evil tempers (the "world," the "flesh," and the "devil"), and the temptations that beset us; conscious that in ourselves we are weak, but that there is a strength greater than our own, "which is perfected in weakness"? Do we think of God as the Eternal, into whose hands our patients, whom we see dying in the Wards, must resign their souls—into whose hands we must resign our own when we depart hence, and ought to resign our own as entirely every morning and night of our lives here; with whom do live the spirits of the just made perfect, with whom do really live, *ought* really as much to live, our spirits here, and who, in the hour of death, in the hour of life, both for our patients and ourselves, must be our trust and hope? We would not always be thinking of death, for "we must live before we die," and life, perhaps, is as difficult as death. Yet the thought of a time when we shall have passed out of the sight and memory of men may also help us to live ; may assist us in shaking off the load of tempers, jealousies, prejudices, bitternesses, interests which weigh us down ; may teach us to rise out of this busy, bustling Hospital world, into the clearer light of God's Kingdom, of which, indeed, this Home is or might be a part, and certainly and especially this Hospital.

This is the spirit of prayer, the spirit of conversation or communion with God, which leads us in all our Nursing silently to think of Him, and refer it to Him. When we hear in the voice of conscience *His* voice speaking to us ; when we are aware that He is the witness of everything we do, and say, and think, and also the source of every good thing in us ; and when we feel in our hearts the struggle against some evil temper, then God is fighting *with* us against envy and jealousy, against selfishness and self-indulgence, against lightness, and frivolity, and vanity, for " our better self against our worse self."

And thus, too, the friendships which have begun at this School may last through life, and be a help and strength to us. For may we not regard the opportunity given for acquiring friends as one of the uses of this place ? and Christian friendship,

D

in uniting us to a friend, as uniting us at the same time to Christ and God ? Christ called His disciples friends, adding the reason, " because He had told them all that He had heard of the Father," just as women tell their whole mind to their friends.

But we all know that there are dangers and disappointments in friendships, especially in women's friendships, as well as joys and sorrows. A woman may have an honourable desire to know those who are her superiors in education, in the School, or in Nursing. Or she may allow herself to drop into the society of those beneath her, perhaps because she is more at home with them, and is proud or shy with her superiors. We do not want to be judges of our fellow-women (for who made thee to differ from another ?), but neither can we leave entirely to chance one of the greatest interests of human life.

True friendship is simple, womanly, unreserved : not weak, or silly, or fond, or noisy, or romping, or extravagant, nor yet jealous and selfish, and exacting more than woman's nature can fairly give, for there are other ties which bind women to one another besides friendship ; nor, again, intrusive into the secrets of another woman, or curious about her circumstances ; rejoicing in the presence of a friend, and not forgetting her in her absence.

Two Probationers or Nurses going together have not only a twofold, but a fourfold strength, if they learn knowledge or good from one another; if they form the characters of one another ; if they support one another in fulfilling the duties and bearing the troubles of a Nursing life, if their friendship thus becomes fellow-service to God in their daily work. They may sometimes rejoice together over the portion of their training which has been accomplished, and take counsel about what remains to be done. They will desire to keep one another up to the mark ; not to allow idleness or eccentricity to spoil their time of training.

But some of our youthful friendships are too violent to last : they have in them something of weakness or sentimentalism ; the feeling passes away, and we become ashamed of them. Or at some critical time a friend has failed to stand by us, and then it is useless to talk of " auld lang syne." Only still let us remember that there are duties which we owe to the " extinct " friend (who perhaps on some fanciful ground has parted company from us), that we should never speak against her, or make use of our knowledge about her. For the memory of a friendship is like the memory of a dead friend, not lightly to be spoken of.

And then there is the " Christian or ideal friendship." What others regard as the service of the sick she may recognise as also the service of God ; what others do out of compassion for their maimed fellow-creatures she may do also for the love of Christ. Feeling that God has made her what she is, she may seek to carry on her work in the Hospital as a fellow-worker with God. Remembering that Christ died for her, she may be ready to lay down her life for her patients.

" They walked together in the house of God as friends "—that is, they served God together in doing good to His sick. For if ever a place may be called the " house of God," it is a Hospital, if it be what it should be. And in old times it *was* called the " house " or the " hotel " of God. The greatest and oldest Central Hospital of Paris, where is the Mother-house of the principal Order of Nursing Sisters, is to this day called the Hôtel Dieu, the " House of God."

There may be some amongst us who, like St. Paul, are capable of feeling a natural interest in

the spiritual welfare of our fellow-probationers—
or, if you like the expression better, in the improvement of their characters—that they may
become more such as God intended them to be in
this Hospital and Home.   For "Christian friendship is not merely the friendship of equals, but of
unequals "—the love of the weak and of those who
can make no return, like the love of God towards
the unthankful and the evil.   It is not a friendship
of one or two but of many.   It proceeds upon a
different rule : "Love your enemies."   It is founded
upon that charity "which is not easily offended,
which beareth all things, believeth all things, hopeth
all things, endureth all things."   Such a friendship
we may be hardly able to reconcile either with our
own character or with common prudence.   Yet
this is the "Christian ideal in the Gospel."   And
here and there may be found some one who has
been inspired to carry out the ideal in practice.

"To live in isolation is to be weak and un-
happy—perhaps to be idle and selfish."   There is
something not quite right in a woman who shuts
up her heart from other women.

This may seem to be telling you what you
already know, and bidding you do what you are
already doing.   Well, then, shall we put the

matter another way ?   Make such friendships as
you will look back upon with pleasure in later
life, and be loyal and true to your friends, not
going from one to another.

> The friends thou hast, and their adoption tried,
> Grapple them to thy soul with hooks of steel ;
> But do not dull thy palm with entertainment
> Of each new-hatched, unfledged comrade.

And do not expect more of them than friends
can give, or weary them with demands for
sympathy ; and do not let the womanliness of
friendship be impaired by any silliness or sentimentalism ; or allow hearty and genial good-will
to degenerate into vulgarity and noise.

And as was once truly said, friendship perhaps
appears best, as it did in St. Paul, in his manner
of rebuking those who had erred, " transferring
their faults in a figure to Apollos and to himself."
" No one knew how to speak the truth in love
like him."

It has been said of Romans xii. : " What rule
of manners can be better than this chapter ?"
" She that giveth, let her do it with simplicity " ;
that is, let us do our acts of Nursing and kindness as if we did not make much of them, as unto
the Lord and not to men.   " Like-minded one

towards another"; that is, we should have the same thoughts and feelings with others. "Rejoicing with them that rejoice, and weeping with them that weep"; going out of ourselves and entering into the thoughts of others.

And have we St. Paul's extraordinary regard for the feelings of others? He was never too busy to think of these. "If meat make my brother to offend, I will eat no more meat while the world standeth," he says, though he well knew such scruples were really superstitions. If the spirit of these words could find a way to our women's hearts, we might be able to say, "See how these Christians (Nurses) love one another!"

Then the courtesy we owe, one woman to another: "for the happiness and the good" of our work and our School is not simply "made up of great duties and virtues, nor the evil of the opposite." But both seem to consist also in a number of small particulars, which, small as they are, have a great effect on the tone and character of our School, introducing light or darkness into the "Home," sweetness or bitterness into our intercourse with one another.

And, as to our Wards: Christ, we may be sure, did not lose authority, or dignity and refinement, "even in the company of publicans and harlots," just as we may observe in the Wards, that there are a few of us whose very refinement makes them do the coarsest and roughest things there with simplicity. A Sister of ours once remarked this of one of her Probationers (who was not a lady in the common sense of the word, but she was the truest gentlewoman in Christ's sense), that she was too refined (most people would have said, to do the indelicate work of the Wards, but *she* said) to see indelicacy in doing the nastiest thing ; and so did it all well, without thinking of herself, or that men's eyes were upon her. That is real dignity—the dignity which Christ had—on which no man can intrude, yet combined with the greatest gentleness and simplicity of life.

II

And let me say a word about self-denial : because, as we all know, there can be no real Nursing without self-denial. We know the story of the Roman soldier, above fourteen hundred years ago, who, entering a town in France with his regiment, saw a sick man perishing with cold by the wayside—there were no Hospitals then—

and, having nothing else to give, drew his sword, cut his own cloak in half, and wrapped the sick man in half his cloak.

It is said that a dream visited him, in which he found himself admitted into heaven, and Christ saying, "Martin hath clothed me with this garment" : the dream, of course, being a remembrance of the verse, "When saw we thee sick or in prison, and came unto thee?" and of the answer, "Inasmuch as ye have done it unto one of the least of these my brethren, ye have done it unto me." But whether the story of the dream be true or not, this Roman soldier, converted to Christianity, became afterwards one of the greatest bishops of the early ages, Martin of Tours.

We are not called upon to feed our patients with our own dinners, or to dress them with our own clothes. We are comfortable, and cannot make ourselves uncomfortable on purpose. But we can learn Sick Cookery for our Patients, we can give up spending our money in foolish dressy ways, and thus squandering what we ought to lay by for ourselves or our families.

On one of the severest winter days in the late war between France and Germany, an immense detachment, many thousands, of wretched French

prisoners were passing through the poorest streets
of one of the largest and poorest German towns
on the way to the prisoners' camp. Every door
in this poor "East End" opened; not one
remained closed; and out of every door came a
poor German woman, carrying in her hand the
dinner or supper she was cooking for herself, her
husband, or children; often all she had in the
house was in her hands. And this she crammed
into the hands of the most sickly-looking prisoner
as he passed by, often into his mouth, as he sank
down exhausted in the muddy street. And the
good-natured German escort, whose business it
was to bring these poor French to their prison,
turned away their heads, and let the women have
their way, though it was late, and they were weary
too. Before the prisoners had been the first hour
in their prison, six had lain down in the straw and
died. But how many lives had been saved that
night by the timely food of these good women,
giving all they had, not of their abundance, but
of their poverty, God only knows, not we. This
was told by an Englishman who was by and saw
it; one of our own "Aid Committee."

And at a large German station, which almost
all the prisoners' trains passed through, a lady

went every night during all that long, long, dreadful winter, and for the whole night, to feed, and warm, and comfort, and often to receive the last dying words of the miserable French prisoners, as they arrived in open trucks, some frozen to the bottom, some only as the dead, others to die in the station, all half-clad and starving. Some had been nine days and nights in these open trucks; many had been twenty-four hours without food. Night after night as these long, terrible trainsful dragged their slow length into the station, she kneeled on its pavement, supporting the dying heads, receiving their last messages to their mothers; pouring wine or hot milk down the throats of the sick; dressing the frost-bitten limbs; and, thank God, saving many. Many were carried to the prisoners' hospital in the town, of whom about two-thirds recovered. Every bit of linen she had went in this way. She herself contracted incurable ill-health during these fearful nights. But thousands were saved by her means.

She is my friend.[1] She came and saw me here after this; and it is from her lips I heard the story. Smallpox and typhus raged among the

[1] Madame Caroline Werckner, an Englishwoman.—EDITOR'S NOTE.

prisoners, most of whom were quite boys. Many were wounded; half were frost-bitten. Sometimes they would snatch at all she brought; but sometimes they would turn away their dying heads from the tempting hot wine, and gasp out, "Thank you, madam; give it to *him*, who wants it more than I." Or, "I'm past help; love to mother."

We have not to give of our own to *our* sick. But shall we the less give them our all—that is, all our hearts and minds? and reasonable service?

Suppose we dedicated this "School" to Him, to the Divine Charity and Love which said, "Inasmuch as ye do it unto one of the least of these my brethren" (and He calls all our patients —all of us, His brothers and sisters) "ye do it unto me"—oh, what a "Kingdom of Heaven" this might be! Then, indeed, the dream of Martin of Tours, the soldier and Missionary-Bishop, would have come true!

III

May I take this opportunity of saying what I think really very much concerns us? First of all, that you have, or might have, directly and indirectly, a great deal to do with maintaining a supply of good candidates to this School. You know whether you have been happy here or not; you know whether you have had opportunities given you here of training and self-improvement. Many, very many of our old Matrons and Nurses have told me that their time as probationers with us was "the happiest time of their lives." It *might* be so with all, though perhaps all do not think so now.

It is in your power to assist the School most materially in obtaining fresh and worthy recruits. There is hardly one of you who has not friends or acquaintances of her own. You *ought* to advertise us. We ought not to have to put one advertisement in the newspapers. If you think this is a worthy life, why do you not bring others to it? I tried to do my part. When Agnes Jones died, though my heart was breaking, I put an article in *Good Words*, such as I knew she would have wished, in all but the mention of herself; and for years her dear memory brought aspirants to the work in our Schools, or others' Schools.

To reform the Nursing of all the Hospitals and Workhouse Infirmaries in the world, and to establish District Nursing among the sick poor at home, too, as at Liverpool—is this not an object most worthy of the co-operation of all civilised people?

In the last ten years, thank God, numerous Training Schools for Nurses have grown up, resolved to unite in putting a stop to such a thing as drunken, immoral, and inefficient Nursing. But all make the same complaint; while the outcry of "employment for women" continues, why does not this most womanly employment for all good women become more sought after? I hope to hear that my old friends in St. Thomas' have each done their part; and I feel quite sure that if it is once placed before them, as a thing they ought to do, they will be found in the front.

You who are assembled in this room, and who are each connected with some circle, directly or indirectly, may do a good work for the civilisation of the Workhouses and Hospitals of the world. If you inform yourselves on the subject, and if you set yourselves to work, to deal with it, as we do with any other great evil that tortures helpless people, you will be able to act directly upon your friends outside, and ultimately get up an amount of public opinion among women capable of becoming Nurses, which will be of the greatest possible aid to our efforts in improving Hospital and Workhouse Nursing. Every one can help— every one—better than if she were a " newspaper," better than if she were a " public meeting." I believe that within a few years you can make it a thing that will be a disgrace to any Hospital or even Workhouse to be suspected of bad Nursing, or to any district (in towns, at any rate) not to have a good District Nurse to nurse the sick poor at home.

Those who have made the right use of all the training that came in their way in this School, if they would write to their own homes for the information of their friends outside, an immense help on its way could be given to the work we have all so much at heart. And I look upon it as a certainty that you will each be able, in one way or another, whether purposely or almost unconsciously, to take a great part in reforming the Hospital and Workhouse Nursing systems of our country, perhaps of our colonies and dependencies, and perhaps of the world.

IV

May I pay ourselves even the least little compliment, as to our being a little less conceited than last year? Were we not as conceited in 1872 as it was possible to be? You shall tell. Are we, in 1873, rather less so? And, without having any one particularly in my head—for what I am going to ask is in fact a truism—is not our conceit always in exact proportion to our ignorance? For those who really know something know how little it is.

Would that this could be a "secret" among us! But, unfortunately, is not our name "up" and "abroad" for conceit? And has it not even been said ("tell it not in Gath") : " And these conceited 'Nightingale' women scarcely know how to read and write ?"

Now let no one look to see our blushes. But shall we not get rid of this which makes us ridiculous as fast as we can?

But enough of this joke ; let us be serious, remembering that the greatest trust which is committed to any woman of us all is, *herself*; and that she is living in the presence of God as well as of her fellow-women.

To know whether we know our Nursing

business or not is a great result of training ; and to think that we know it when we do *not* is as great a proof of want of training.

The world, more especially the Hospital world, is in such a hurry, is moving so fast, that it is too easy to slide into bad habits before we are aware. And it is easier still to let our year's training slip away without forming any real plan of training ourselves.

For, after all, all that any training is to do for us is : to teach us how to train ourselves, how to observe for ourselves, how to think out things for ourselves. Don't let us allow the first week, the second week, the third week to pass by—I will not say in idleness, but in bustle. Begin, for instance, at once making notes of your cases. From the first moment you see a case, you can observe it. Nay, it is one of the first things a Nurse is strictly called upon to do : to observe her sick. Mr. Croft has taught you how to take notes ; and you have now, every one of you, two leisure times a week to work up your notes.

But give but one-quarter of an hour a *day* to jot down, even in words which no one can understand but yourself, the progress or change of two or three individual cases, not to forget or confuse

E

them. You can then write them out at your two
leisure times. To those who have not much
education, I am sure that our kind Home Sister,
or the Special Probationer in the same Ward, or
nearest in any way, will give help. The race is
not always to the swift, nor the battle to the strong ;
and "line upon line"—*one* line every day—in the
steady, observing, humble Nurse has often won the
race over the smarter "genius" in what constitutes
real Nursing. But few of us women seriously think
of improving our own mind or character *every day.*
And this is fatal to our improving in Nursing. We
do not calculate the future by our experience of the
past. What right have we to expect that, if we
have not improved during the last six months, we
shall during the next six? Then, we do not allow
for the changes which circumstances make in us—
the being put on Staff duty, when we certainly shall
not have more time, but less, for improving ourselves, or the growing older or more feeble in
health. We believe that we shall always have the
same powers or opportunities for learning our
business which we now have. Our time of training
slips away in this unimproving manner. And when
a woman begins to see how many things might have
been better in her, she is too old to change, or it is

too late, too late. And she confesses to herself, or oftener she does not confess—"How all her life she had been in the wrong."

We are all of us, as we believe, passing into an unknown world, of which this is only a part. We have been here a year, or part of a year. What are we making of our own lives? Are we where we were a year ago? Or are we fitter for that work of after-life which we have undertaken?

Do our faults, and weaknesses, and vanities, tend to diminish? Or are we still listless, inefficient, slow, bustling, conceited, unkind, hard judges of others, instead of helping them where we can? There is no greater softener of hard judgments than is the trying to help the person whom we so judge, as I can tell from my own experience; and in this you will tell me whether we have been deficient to each other. There is a true story told of Captain Marryat when a boy; that he jumped overboard to save an older midshipman who had made the boy's life a misery to him by his filthy cruelties. And the boy Marryat wrote home to his mother "that he loved this midshipman now —and wasn't it lucky that his life was saved—even better than his own darling mother."

Do we keep before our minds constantly the

sense of our duty here, of our duty to others—Nurses, Sisters, Matron—as well as to ourselves, our fellow Probationers, and our Home Sister, and to the whole School of which we are members ?

If we thought of this more, we might hope to attain that quiet mind and self-control, which is the "liberty" spoken of by St. Paul. We might learn how truly to use and enjoy both our fellow Probationers, and this Home and our School, if we were more anxious about following the example of Christ than about the opinion of our "world." " We are the 'world,' which we often seem to think includes every one but *us*."

But few comparatively have the power of disengaging themselves, even in thought, from those about them. They take the view of their own set. If it is the fashion to conceal, they conceal ; if to carry tales, they carry tales. There are a few who never allow themselves to speak against others, and exercise such a kind of authority as to prevent others being spoken against in their hearing. These are the "peacemakers" of whom Christ speaks. These are they who keep a Home or Institution together, and seem more than any others in this our little world to bear the image of Christ until His coming again.

Do we ever do things because they are right, without regard to our own credit? When we ask ourselves only "What is right?" or (which is the same question), "What is the will of God?" then we are truly entering His "kingdom." We are no longer grovelling among the opinions of men and women. We can see God in all things, and all things in God, the Eternal Father shining through the accidents of our lives—which sometimes shake us more, though less conspicuous, than the accidents we see brought in to our Surgical Wards—the accidents of the characters of those under whom we are placed, and of our own inner life.

One of the greatest missionaries that ever was, wrote more than 300 years ago to his pupils and fellow-missionaries :

"Self-knowledge "—(the knowledge by which we see ourselves in God)—"self-knowledge is the nurse of confidence in God. It is from distrust of ourselves that confidence in God is born. This will be the way for us to gain that true interior lowliness of mind which, in all places, and especially here, is far more necessary than you think. I warn you also not to let the good opinion which men have of you be too much of a pleasure to you, unless perhaps in order that you may be the more

ashamed of yourselves on that account.   It is that
which leads people to neglect themselves, and this
negligence, in many cases, upsets, *as by a kind of trick*,
all that lowliness of which I speak, and puts conceit
and arrogance in its place.   And thus so many do
not see for a long time how much they have lost,
and gradually lose all care for piety, and all tran-
quillity of mind, and thus are always troubled and
anxious, finding no comfort either from without or
within themselves."

"Come unto me, all ye that labour and are heavy
laden," says our Lord, "and I will give you rest."
But He adds immediately who those are to whom
He will give this "rest" or quietness of mind—
namely those, who, like Himself, are "meek and
lowly of heart."

These words may seem in a Hospital life "like
dreams."   But they are not dreams if we take them
for the spirit of our School and the rule of our
Nursing.   "To practise them, to feel them, to
make them our own," this is not far from the
"kingdom of Heaven" in a Hospital.

Pray for me, as I do for you, that "piety" and
a "quiet mind"—but these always and only in the
strenuous effort to *press forwards*—may be ours.

FLORENCE NIGHTINGALE.

III

ANOTHER year has passed over us, my dear friends. There have been many changes among us. We have each of us tasted somewhat more of the discipline of life. To some of us it may have been very bitter ; to others, let us hope, not so. By all, let us trust, it has been put to heroic uses.

"Heroic ? " I think I hear you say ; " can there be much of ' heroic ' in washing porringers and making beds ? "

I once heard a man (he is dead now) giving a lesson to some poor orphan girls in an Orphan Asylum. Few things, I think, ever struck me so much, or them. It was on the " heroic virtues." It went into the smallest particulars of thrift, of duty, of love and kindness ; and he ended by asking them how they thought such small people as themselves could manage to practise those great virtues. A child of seven put up its little nib and

55

chirped out : " Please, my lord, we might pick up pins when we don't like to." That showed she understood his lesson.

His lesson was not exactly fitted to us, but we may all fit it to ourselves.

This night, if we are inclined to make a noise on the stairs, or to linger in each other's rooms, shall we go quietly to bed, alone with God? Some of you yourselves have told me that you could get better day sleep in the Night Nurses' Dormitory than in your own "Home." Is there such loud laughing and boisterous talking in the daytime, going upstairs to your rooms, that it disturbs any one who is ill, or prevents those who have been on night duty from getting any sleep ?

Is that doing what you would be done by— loving your neighbour as yourselves, as our Master told us ?

Do you think it is we who invent the duty " Quiet and orderly," or is it He ?

If our uniform dress is not what we like, shall we think of our Lord, whose very garments were divided by the soldiers ? (But I always think how much more becoming is our uniform than any other dress I see.)

If there is anything at table that we don't like,

shall we take it thankfully, remembering Who had to ask a poor woman for a drink of water?

Shall we take the utmost pains to be perfectly regular and punctual to all our hours—going into the wards, coming out of the wards, at meals, etc.? And if we are unavoidably prevented, making an apology to the Home Sister, remembering what has been written about those who are in authority over us? Or do we think a few minutes of no consequence in coming from or going to the wards?

Do we carefully observe our Rules?

If we *are* what is printed at the top of our Duties, viz. :

> Trustworthy,
> Punctual,
> Quiet and orderly,
> Cleanly and neat,
> Patient, cheerful, and kindly,

we scarcely need any other lesson but what explains these to us.

Trustworthy : that is, faithful.

Trustworthy when we have no one by to urge or to order us. " Her lips were never opened but to speak the truth." Can that be said of us?

Trustworthy, in keeping our soul in our hands, never excited, but always ready to lift it up to

God ; unstained by the smallest flirtation, innocent of the smallest offence, even in thought.

Trustworthy, in doing our work as faithfully as if our superiors were always near us.

Trustworthy, in never prying into one another's concerns, but ever acting behind another's back as one would to her face.

Trustworthy, in avoiding every word that could injure, in the smallest degree, our patients, or our companions, who are our neighbours, remembering how St. Peter says that God made us *all* "stewards of grace one to another."

How can we be "stewards of grace" to one another ? By giving the "grace" of our good example to all around us. And how can we become "untrustworthy stewards" to one another? By showing ourselves lax in our habits, irregular in our ways, not doing as we should do if our superiors were by. "Cripple leads the way." Shall the better follow the worse ?

It has happened to me to hear some of you say —perhaps it has happened to us all—"Indeed, I only did what I saw done."

How glorious it would be if " only doing what we saw done" always led us right !

A master of a great public school once said that

he could trust his whole school, because he could trust every single boy in it. Oh, could God but say that He can trust this Home and Hospital because He can trust every woman in it ! Let us try this—every woman to work as though success depended on herself. Do you know that, in this great Indian Famine, every Englishman has worked as if success depended on himself ? And in saving a population as large as that of England from death by starvation, do you not think that we have achieved the greatest victory we ever won in India ? Suppose we work thus for this Home and Hospital.

Oh, my dear friends, how terrible it will be to any one of us, some day, to hear another say, that she only did what she saw us do, if that was on the "road that leadeth to destruction" !

Or taking it another way, how delightful—how delightful to have set another on her journey to heaven by our good example ; how terrible to have delayed another on her journey to heaven by our bad example !

There is an old story—nearly six hundred years old—when a ploughboy said to a truly great man, whose name is known in history, that he "advised" him "always to live in such a way that those who had a good opinion of him might never be disappointed."

The great man thanked him for his advice, and —kept it.

If our School has a good name, do we live so that people "may never be disappointed" in its Nurses?

Obedient : not wilful : not having such a sturdy will of our own. Common sense tells us that no training can do us any good, if we are always seeking our own way. I know that some have really sought in dedication to God to give up their own wills to His. For if you enter this Training School, is that not in effect a promise to Him to give up your own way for that way which you are taught?

Let us not question so much. You *must* know that things have been thought over and arranged for your benefit. You are not bound to think us always right : perhaps you can't. But are *you* more likely to be right? And, at all events, you know you *are* right, if you choose to enter our ways, to submit yours to them.

In a foreign Training School, I once heard a most excellent pastor, who was visiting there, say to a nurse: " Are you *dis*couraged?—say rather, you are *dis*obedient : they always mean the same thing." And I thought how right he was. And, what is more, the Nurse thought so too ; and she was not "discouraged" ever after, because she gave up being "disobedient."

"Every one for herself" ought to have no footing here : and these strong wills of ours God will teach. If we do not let Him teach us here, He will teach us by some sterner discipline hereafter—teach our wills to bend first to the will of God, and then to the reasonable and lawful wills of those among whom our lot is cast.

I often say for myself, and I have no doubt you do, that line of the hymn :

Tell me, Thou yet wilt chide, Thou canst not spare,
O Lord, Thy chastening rod.

Let Him reduce us to His discipline before it is too late. If we "kick against the pricks," we can only pray that He will give us more "pricks," till we cease to "kick." And it is a proof of His fatherly love, and that He has not given us up, if He does.

For myself, I can say that I have never known what it was, since I can remember anything, not to have "prickly" discipline, more than any one knew of ; and I hope I have not "kicked."

To return to *Trustworthiness.*

Most of you, on leaving the Home, go first on

night duty.   Now there is nothing like night duty for trying our trustworthiness.   A year hence you will tell me whether you have felt any temptation not to be quite honest in reporting cases the next morning to your Sister or Nurse : that is, to say you have observed when you have not observed ; to slur over things in your report, which, for aught you know, may be of consequence to the patient : to slur over things in your work because there is no one watching you : no one but God.

It has indeed been known that the Night Nurse had stayed in the kitchen to talk ; but we may trust such things will not happen again.

And, for all, let us *all* say this word for ourselves : everything gets toppled over if we don't make it a matter of conscience, a matter of reckoning between ourselves and our God.   That is the only safeguard of real *trustworthiness*.   If we treat it as a mere matter of business, of success in our career in life, never shall we give anything but eye-service, never shall we be really trustworthy.

Orderly : Let us never waste anything, even pins or paper, as some do, by beginning letters or resolutions, or " cases," which they never take the trouble to finish.

Cheerful and Patient : Let us never wish for

more than is necessary, and be cheerful when what we should like is sometimes denied us, as it may be some day ; or when people are unkind, or we are disregarded by those we love : remembering Him whose attendants at His death were mocking soldiers.

I assure you, my friends, that if we can practise those "duties" faithfully, we are practising the "heroic virtues."

Patient, cheerful, and kindly : Now, is it being patient, cheerful, and kindly to be so only with those who are so to us? For, as St. Peter tells us, even ungodly people do that. But if we can do good to some one who has done us ill, oh, what a privilege that is! And even God will thank us for it, the Apostle says. Let us be kindest to the impatient and unkindly.

Now let me tell you of two Nurses whom we knew.

One was a lady, with just enough to live upon, who took an old widow to nurse into her house : recommended to her by her minister. One day she met him and reproached him. Why? Because the old widow was "too good" ; "*any* body could nurse *her*." Presently a grumbling old woman, never contented with anything anybody did,

who thought she was never treated well enough,
and that she never had "her due," was found.
And this old woman the lady took into her house
and nursed till she died ; because, she said, nobody
else liked to do anything for her, and *she* did.
That was something like kindness, for there is no
great kindness in doing good to any one who is
grateful and thanks us for it.

But my other story is something much better
still.

A poor Nurse, who had been left a widow, with
nothing to live upon but her own earnings, in-
quired for some *tedious children* to take care of.
As you may suppose, there was no difficulty in
finding this article. And from that day, for twenty
years, she never had less than two, three, or four
orphans with her, and sometimes five, whom she
brought up as her own, training them for service.
She taught them domestic work, for she herself
went out to service at nine years old. She never
had any difficulty in finding places for them, and
for twenty years she had thus a succession of
children. But she taught them something better.

She taught them that they had "nothing but
their character to depend upon." " I tell them,"
she said, " it was all I had myself; God helps girls

that watch over themselves. If a girl isn't made to feel this early, it's hard afterwards to make her feel it."

These girls, so brought up, turned out much better than those brought up in most large Union schools, for asylums are not like homes. Of the children whom Nurse took in, one was a girl of such bad habits and such a mischief-maker that no one else could manage her. But Nurse did. She soon found she could not refuse boys. One was a boy of fourteen, just out of prison for bad ways, whom she took and reclaimed, and who became as good a boy as can be. These are only two specimens.

They called her "Mother." And God, she used to say, gave them to her as her own. You will ask how she supported them. The larger number of them she supported by taking in washing, by charing one day a week, and bye and bye, by taking in journeymen as lodgers. Now and then a lady would pay for an orphan. Once she took in a sailor's five motherless children for 5s. a week from the father : but she has taken in apprentices as lodgers, whose own fathers could not afford to keep them for their wages.

All this time she washed for a poor sick Irish-woman, who never gave her any thanks but that

F

"the clothes were not well washed, nor was anything done as it ought to be done." Yet she took in this woman's child of two years old as her own, till the father came back, when he gave up drink and claimed it.

Every Friday she gave her earnings to some poor women, who bought goods with the money, which they sold again in the market on Saturday, and returned her money to her on Saturday night. She said she never lost a penny by this: and it kept several old women going.

She must have been a capital manager, you will say. Well, till she took in lodgers, she lived in a cellar which she painted with her own hands, and kept as clean as a new pin. Afterwards she let her cellar for 2s. a week, though she might have got 2s. 6d. or 3s. a week for it, because, she said, "the poor should not be hard on one another." Milk she never tasted ; meat seldom, and then she always stewed, never roasted it. She lived on potatoes, and potato pie was the luxury of herself and children.

On Sundays she filled her pot of four gallons and made broth : sometimes for six or eight poor old women besides her own family, as she called her orphans. *These* must be satisfied with what she provided, little or much. She never let them touch what was sent her for her patients. Sometimes good things were sent her, which she always gave to sick neighbours ; yet she has been accused of keeping for herself nice things sent to her care for others. She never owed a penny, for all her charity.

If this Nurse has not practised the " heroic virtues," who has ?

I mentioned this Nurse merely as an instance of one who literally fulfilled the precept to " do good " to them that " despitefully use you " : to be " patient, cheerful, and kindly." There is no time to tell you how she was left a widow with two infants and a blind and insane mother, whom she kept till doctors compelled her to put her mother into a lunatic asylum : how one of her sons was a sickly cripple, whom she nursed till he died, working by day and sitting up with him at night for years : how the other boy was insane, and ran away : how, to ease her broken mother's heart, she returned to sick-nursing, chiefly among the poor, nursed through two choleras, till her health broke down, and, by way of taking care of herself, then took up the " tedious " orphan system, which she never ceased. She felt, she said, as if she were doing something then for her "own dear boy." As soon as she lived in a poor house of four rooms and an attic, she has had as many as ten carpenters' men of a night, who had nowhere but the public-house to go to. She gave them a good fire, borrowed a newspaper for them, and made one read aloud. They brought her sixpence a week, and she laid it all out in supper for them, and cooked it. She gave the only good pair of shoes she had to one of these, because " he must go to work decent! "

She was a famous sick cook, often carrying home fish-bones to stew them for the sick, who seldom thanked her ; and the remains of damsons and currants, to boil over again as a drink for fever patients . who sometimes accused her of keeping back things sent for them.

" How much more the Lord has borne from me," she used to say.

And of children she used to say : " We never can train up a child in the way it should go till we take it in our arms, as Jesus did, and feel : ' Of such is the kingdom of heaven ' ; and that there is a 'heavenly principle' (a 'little angel,' I think she said) in each child to be trained up in it."

She said she had learnt this from the master in a factory where she had once nursed.

(How little he knew that he had been one means of forming this heroic Nurse.)

II

And now I have a word for the Ladies, and a word for the Nurse - Probationers. Which shall come first?

Do the ladies follow up their intellectual privileges? Or, are they lazy in their hours of study? Do they cultivate their powers of expression in answering Mr. Croft's examinations?

Ought they not to look upon themselves as future leaders — as those who will have to train others? And to bear this in mind during the whole of their year's training, so as to qualify themselves for being so? It is not just getting through the year anyhow, without being blamed. For the year leaves a stamp on everybody—this for the Nurses as well as the Ladies—and once gone can never be regained.

To the Special Probationers may I say one more word?

Do we look enough into the importance of

giving ourselves thoroughly to study in the hours
of study, of keeping careful *Notes of Lectures*, of
keeping notes of all type cases, and of cases
interesting from not being type cases, so as to
improve our powers of observation—all essential
if we are in future to have charge ? Do we keep
in view the importance of helping ourselves to
understand these cases by reading at the time books
where we can find them described, and by listening
to the remarks made by Physicians and Surgeons
in going round with their Students? (Take a
sly note afterwards, when nobody sees, in order
to have a correct remembrance.)

So shall we do everything in our power to
become proficient, not only in knowing the
symptoms and what is to be done, but in knowing
the " Reason Why " of such symptoms, and *why*
such and such a thing is done ; and so on, till we
can some day TRAIN OTHERS *to know the " reason
why*."

Many say : " We have no time ; the Ward
work gives us no time."

But it is so easy to degenerate into a mere
drudgery about the Wards, when we have goodwill
to do it, and are fonder of practical work than
of giving ourselves the trouble of learning the

" reason why." Take care, or the Nurses, some of them, will catch you up.

Take ten minutes a day in the Ward to jot down things, and write them out afterwards : come punctually *from* your Ward to have time for doing so. *It is far better to take these ten minutes to write your cases or to jot down your recollections in the Ward than to give the same ten minutes to bustling about.* I am sure the Sisters would help you to get this time if you asked them : and also to *leave* the Ward punctually.

And do you not think this a religious duty?

Such observations are a religious meditation : for is it not the best part of religion to imitate the benevolence of God to man? And how can you do this—in this your calling especially—if you do not thoroughly understand your calling? And is not every study to do this a religious contemplation?

Without it, *May you not potter and cobble about the patients without ever once learning the reason of what you do, so as to be able to train others?*

(I do not say anything about the " cards," for I take it for granted that you can read them easily.)

Our dear Matron, who is always thinking of

arranging for us, is going to have a case-paper with printed headings given to you, and to keep this correctly ought to be a mere every-day necessity, and a very easy one, for you.

2. And for the Nurses :

They are placed, perhaps here only, on a footing of equality with educated gentlewomen. Do they show their appreciation of this by thinking, " We are as good as they " ? Or, by obedience and respect, and trying to profit by the superior education of the gentlewomen ?

Both we have known ; we have known Nurse-Probationers who took the Ladies " under their protection " in saving them the harder work, and the Ladies have given them the full return back in helping them in their education.

And we have known—very much the reverse.

Also, do the Nurse-Probationers take advantage of their opportunities, in the excellent classes given them by the Home Sister, in keeping diaries and some cases ?

Very few of the Nurse-Probationers have taken notes of Mr. Croft's Lectures at all ; it is not fair to Mr. Croft to give him people who do not benefit by his instruction.

3. And I have another word to say :

Are there parties in our Home?

Could we but be *not* so tenacious of our own interests, but look at the thing in a larger way!

Is there a great deal of canvassing and misinterpreting Sisters and Matron and other authorities? every little saying and doing of theirs? talking among one another about the superiors (and then finding we were all wrong when we came to know them better)?

We must all of us know, without being told, that we cannot be trained at all, if in training this will of our own is not kept under.

Do not question so much. Does not a spirit of criticism go with ignorance? Are some of you in all the " opposition of irresponsibility " ? Some day, when you are yourselves responsible, you will know what I mean.

Now could not the Ladies help the Nurse-Probationers in this : (1) in never themselves criticising ; and (2) in saying a kindly word to check it when it is done?

Let me tell you a true story about this.

In a large college, questions—about things which the students could but imperfectly understand in the conduct of the college—had become too warm. The superintendent went into the hall one morning, and after complimenting the young men on their studies, he said : " This morning I heard two of the porters, while at their work, take up a Greek book lying on my table ; one tried to read it, and the other declared it ought to be held upside down to be read. Neither could agree which *was* upside down, but both thought themselves quite capable of arguing about Greek, though neither could read it. They were just coming to fisticuffs, when I sent the two on different errands."

Not a word was added : the students laughed and retired, but they understood the moral well enough, and from that day there were few questions or disputes about the plans and superiors of the college, or about their own obedience to rules and discipline.

Do let us think of the two porters squabbling whether the Greek book was to be read upside down, when we feel inclined to be questioning about " things too high for us."

We are constantly making mistakes in our judgment of our little world. We fancy that we have been harshly treated or misunderstood. Or we cannot bear our fellow-Probationers to laugh at us.

Believe me, there will come a time when all such troubles will simply seem ridiculous to us, and we shall be unable to imagine how we could ever have been the victims of them. (One of your number told me this herself. She has left St. Thomas' for another post.) Let us not brood or sentimentalise over them. They should be met in a common-sense way. How much of our time has been spent in grieving over these trifles, how little in the real sorrow for sin, the real struggle for improvement.

4. As for obedience to rules and our superiors : "True obedience," said one of the most efficient people who ever lived, " obeys not only the command, but also the intention " of those who have a right to command us. Of course, this is a truism : the thing is, *how to do it*. As it is a struggle, it requires a brave and intrepid spirit, which helps us to rise above trifles and look to God, and His leadings for us. Oh, when death comes, how sorry we shall be to have watched others so much and ourselves so little ; to have dug so much in the field of others' consciences and left our own fallow ! What should we say of a " Leopold " Nurse who should try to nurse in "Edward" Ward, and neglect her own "Leopold" ?

Well, that is what we do. Or who should wash her patients' hands and not her own ?

It is of ourselves and not of others that we must give an account. Let us look to our own consciences as we do to our own hands, to see if they are dirty.

We take care of our dress, but do we take care of our words ?

It is a very good rule to say and do nothing but what we can offer to God. Now we cannot offer Him backbiting, petty scandal, misrepresentation, flirtation, injustice, bad temper, bad thoughts, jealousy, murmuring, complaining. Do we ever think that we bear the responsibility of all the harm we do in this way ?

Look at that busybody who fidgets, gossips, makes a bustle, always wanting to domineer, always thinking of herself, as if she wanted to tell the sun to get out of her way and let her light the world in its place, as the proverb says.

And when we might do all our actions and say all our words as unto God !

So many imperfections; so many thoughts of self-love ; so many selfish satisfactions that we mix with our best actions ! And when we might offer them all to God. What a pity !

5. One word more for the Ladies, or those who will have to train and look after others.

What must she be who is to be a Ward or " Home " Sister?

We see her in her nobleness and simplicity : being, not seeming : without name or reward in this world : " clothed " in her " righteousness " merely, as the Psalms would say, *not* in her dignity : often having no gifts of money, speech, or strength : but never preferring seeming to being.

And if she rises still higher, she will find herself, in some measure, like the Great Example in Isaiah liii., bearing the sins and sorrows of others as if they were her own : her counsels often " despised and rejected," yet " opening not her mouth " to be angry : " led as a lamb to the slaughter."

She who rules best is she who loves best : and shows her love not by foolish indulgence to those of whom she is in charge, but by taking a real interest in them for their own sakes, and in their highest interests.

Her firmness must never degenerate into nervous irritability. And for this end let me advise you when you become Sisters, always to take your exercise time out of doors, your monthly day out, and your annual holiday.

Be a judge of the work of others of whom you are in charge, not a detective : your mere detective "is wonderful at suspicion and discovery," but is often at fault, foolishly imagining that every one is bad.

The Head-Nurse must have been tested in the refiner's fire, as the prophets would say : have been tried by many tests : and have come out of them stainless, in full command of herself and her principles : never losing her temper.

She never nurses well till she ceases to command for the sake of commanding, or for her own sake at all : till she nurses only for the sakes of those who are nursed. This is the highest exercise of self-denial ; but without it the ruin of the nursing, of the charge, is sure to come.

Have we ever known such a Nurse ?

She must be just, not unjust.

Now justice is the perfect order by which every woman does her own business, and injustice is where every woman is doing another's business. This is the most obvious of all things : and for that very reason has never been found out. Injustice is the habit of being a busybody and doing another woman's business, which tries to rule and ought to serve : this is the unjust Nurse.

Prudence is doing your nursing most perfectly : aiming at the perfect in everything : this is the "seeking God and His righteousness" of the Scriptures.

And must not each of us be a Saviour, rather than a ruler : each in our poor measure ? Did the Son of God try to rule ? Oh, my friends, do not scold at women : they will be of another mind if they are "gently entreated" and learn to know you. Who can hate a woman who loves them ? Or be jealous of one who has no jealousy ? Who can squabble with one who never squabbles ? It is example which converts your patients, your ward-maids, your fellow-Nurses or charges : it is example which converts the world.

And is not the Head-Nurse or Sister there, not that she may do as she likes, but that she should serve all for the common good of all? The one worst maxim of all for a future Matron, Sister, or Nurse is "to do as I like" : that *is* disorder, not rule. It is giving power to evil.

Those who rule must not be those who are desirous to rule.

She who is best fitted is often the least inclined

to rule : but if the necessity is laid upon her, she takes it up as a message from God. And she must no longer live in her own thoughts, making a heaven or hell of her own. For if she does not make a heaven for others, her charge will soon become something else.

She must never become excited : and therefore I do impress upon you regularity and punctuality, and never to get hurried. Those often get most excited who are least in earnest. She who is fierce with her Nurses, her patients, or her ward-maid, is not truly above them : she is below them : and, although a harsh ward-mistress to her patients or Nurses, has no real superiority over them.

There is no impudence like that of ignorance. Each night let us come to a knowledge of ourselves before going to rest : as the Psalm says : " Commune with your own heart upon your bed, *and be still*." Is it possible that we who live among the sick and dying can be satisfied not to make *friends* with *God* each night ?

The future Sister should be neither mistress nor servant, but the *friend* of every woman under her. If she is mistress of others when she is not mistress of herself, her jealous, faithless temper grows worse with command (oh, let not this be the case with any of us!)—wanting everything of everybody, yet not knowing how to get it of anybody. Always in fear, confusion, suspicion, and distraction, she becomes more and more faithless, envious, unrighteous, the cause of wretchedness to herself and others. She who has no control over herself, who cannot master her own temper, how can she be placed over others, to control them through the better principle? But she who is the most royal mistress of herself is the only woman fit to be in charge.

For this is the whole intention of training, education, supervision, superintendence : to give self-control, to train or nurse up in us a higher principle ; and when this is attained, you may go your ways safely into the world.

But she who nurses, and does not nurse up in herself the " infant Christ," who should be born again in us every day, is like an empty syringe— it pumps in only wind.

The future Sister must be not of the governessing but of the Saviour turn of mind.

Let her reason with the unjust woman who is not intentionally in error. She must know how to give good counsel, which will advise what is

G

best under the circumstances ; not making a
lament, but finding a cure ; regarding *that* only
as "bettering" their situation which *makes them
better*. She must know and teach "how to refuse
the evil and choose the good," as Isaiah says.

She must have an iron sense of truth and right
for herself and others, and a golden sense of love
and charity for them.

When a future Sister unites the power of command with the power of thought and love, when
she can raise herself and others above the common-
places of a common self without disregarding any
of our common feelings, when she can plan and
effect any reforms wanted step by step, without
trying to precipitate them into a single year or
month, neither hasting nor delaying : that is
indeed a "Sister."

The future Sister or Head must not see only a
little corner of things, her own petty likes and
dislikes ; she must "lift up her eyes to the hills,"
as David says. She must know that there is a
greater and more real world than her own little-
nesses and meannesses. And she must be not only
the friend of her Nurses, but also, in her measure,
the angel whose mission is to reconcile her Nurses
to themselves, to each other, and to God.

III

Now let us not each of us think how this fits on to her neighbour, but how it fits on to oneself.

Shall I tell you what one of you said to me after I last addressed you?—"Do you think we are missionaries?"

I answer, that you cannot help being missionaries, if you would. There are missionaries for evil as well as for good. Can you help choosing? Must you not decide whether you will be missionaries for good, or whether for evil, among your patients and among yourselves?

And, first, among your patients:

Hospital Nurses have charge of their patients in a way that no other woman has charge; in the first place, no other woman is in charge really of grown-up men. Oh, how careful she ought to be, especially the Night Nurse, to show them what a true woman can be! The acts of a nurse are keenly scrutinised by both old and young patients. If she is not perfectly pure and upright, depend upon it, they know.

Also, a Hospital Nurse is in charge of people in their sick and feeble, anxious and dying hours, when they are singularly alive to impressions. She leaves her stamp upon them, whether she will or no. And this applies almost more to the Night Nurse than to the Day Nurse.

Lastly, if she have children-patients, she is absolutely in charge of these, who come, perhaps for the first and the last time of their lives, under influence.

So many pass by a child without notice. A whole life of happiness or wretchedness may turn upon an act of kindness to it—a good example set it. A poor woman once said of a child of hers under just these circumstances : "The Sister set its face heavenwards: and it never looked back." Do we ever set their faces the other way ? The child she spoke of when it was dying actually gave its halfpence, which it had saved for something for itself, for another dying child "who had nobody." I call *that* practising the "heroic virtues," if ever there were such. And that was done under just such an influence as we have been speaking of.

On the other hand, do you know anything in its way more heinous than a Nurse, who to the sick and tiresome child might be like an angel "to set it face heavenward" by her sympathy with it, and who, by her own bad habits or bad temper, by her unfairness, by her unkindness or injustice, by her coarseness or want of uprightness, sets it the other way ?

A very good man once said that in each little Hospital patient, he saw not only a soul to be saved, but many other souls that might possibly be committed to this one : for the poor can do so much among one another : do what no others going among them can do. Every child is of the stuff out of which Home Missionaries may be made, such as God chooses from the ranks that have furnished his best recruits.

The Apostles were fishermen and workmen.

David Livingstone was a cotton-mill piecer. In each little pauper waif he saw one destined to carry a godly example (or the reverse) where none but they could carry it—into godless and immoral homes.

We will not repeat here, because we are so fully persuaded of it, that a woman, especially a Nurse, must be a missionary, *not* as a minister or chaplain is, but by the influence of her own character, silent but not unfelt.

It was this, far more than any words, that gave his matchless influence to David Livingstone, whose body, brought upwards of 1500 miles through pathless deserts by his own negro servants—such a heroic feat as Christians never knew before—was buried this spring in Westminster Abbey. Some of us knew him : one of our Probationers was with him and his wife, who died in 1862, and Bishop Mackenzie, at their Mission Station in Africa. He was such a traveller and missionary as we shall never see again perhaps. But what he was in influence each of us may be, if we please, in our little sphere.

A Nurse *is* like a traveller, from the quantity of people who pass before her in the ever-changing wards. And she is like a traveller also in this, that, as Livingstone used to say, either the vices or the virtues of civilisation follow the footsteps of the traveller, and he cannot help it. So they do those of the Nurse. And missioning will be, whether she will or no, the background of her nursing, as it is the background of travelling. The traveller may call himself a missionary or not, as he likes. He *is* one, for good or for evil. So is the Nurse.

Livingstone used to say that we fancy a missionary a man with a Bible in his hand and another in his pack. He then went on to say what a real missionary must be in himself to have influence. And he added : " If I had once been suspected of a single act of want of purity or uprightness the negroes would never have trusted me again. No, not even the least pure or the least upright of the negroes. And any influence of mine would have been gone for ever." What his influence was, even after his death, you know.

Then you must be missionaries, whether you will or no, among one another.

We need only think of the friendships that are made here. Will you be a missionary of good or of evil to your friend? Will you be a missionary of indifference, selfishness, lightness of conduct, self-indulgence? Or a missionary—to her and to your patients—of religious and noble devotion to duty, carried out to the smallest thing?

Will you be a "hero" in your daily work, like the dying child giving its hard-saved halfpence to the yet poorer child?

Livingstone always remembered that a poor old Scotchman on his death-bed had said to him: "Now, lad, make religion the *every-day* business of your life, not a thing of fits and starts; for if you do not, temptation and other things will get the better of you."

Such a Nurse—one who makes religion the " every-day business of her life," *is* a "Missionary," even if she never speak a word. One who does not is a missionary for *evil* and not for good, though she may say many words, have many good texts at the end of her tongue, or, as Livingstone would say, a Bible in her hand and a Bible at her back.

Believe me, who have seen a good deal of the world, we may give you an institution to learn in, but it is You must furnish the " heroic" feeling of doing your duty, doing your best, without which no institution is safe, without which Training Schools are meat without salt. *You* must be our salt, without which civilisation is but corruption, and all churches only dead establishments.

Shall I tell you what one of the most famous clergymen that ever lived said ? That, in order to manage people, and especially children, well, it was necessary to speak more of them to God than of God to them. If a famous preacher said that, how much more must a woman ?

Another learned clergyman, who was also the best translator of the Bible (in a foreign language), said: " Prayer, rather than speech must be relied upon for the reform of any little irregularities: for only through prayer could the proper moment for speech become known." If a great leader of mankind said that, how much more should a Nurse ?

I must end : and what I say now I had better have said : and nothing else.

What are we without God ? Nothing.

" Father, glorify Thy name ! " How is His name glorified ? *We* are His glory, when we follow His ways. Then we are something.

What is the Christian religion ? To be like Christ.

And what is it to be like Christ ? To be High Church, Low Church, Dissenter, or orthodox ? Oh, no. It is : to live for God and have God for our object.

IV

LONDON, *May* 26, 1875.

MY DEAR FRIENDS,—This year my letter to you must needs be short, for I am not able to write much. But good words are always short. The best words that ever were spoken—Christ's words —were the shortest. Would that ours were always the echo of His !

First, then :

What is our one thing needful ? To have high principles at the bottom of all. Without this, without having laid our foundation, there is small use in building up our details. That is as if you were to try to nurse without eyes or hands. We know who said, If your foundation is laid in shifting sand, you may build your house, but it will tumble down. But if you build it on solid ground, this is what is called being *rooted and grounded in Christ*.

In the great persecutions in France two hundred

years ago (not only of the Protestants, who came over here and settled in Spitalfields, but of all who held the higher and more spiritual religion) a noble woman, who has left her impress on the Christian Church, and who herself endured two hard imprisonments for conscience' sake, would receive no Probationer into her Institution, which was, like ours, for works of Nursing and for the poor, till the Probationer had well considered whether she were really rooted and grounded in God himself, and not in the mere habit of obeying rule and doing her work ; whether she could do without the supports of the example and fellowship of a large and friendly community, the sympathy and praise of fellow-workers—all good things in themselves, but which will not carry us through a life like Christ's. And I doubt whether any woman whom God is forming for Himself is not at some time or other of her life tried and tested in this lonely path.

A French Princess, who did well consider, and who was received into the said Institution on these conditions, has left us in writing her experience. And well she showed *where* she was " rooted and grounded " through ten after-years of prison and persecution.

We have not to endure these things. Our lot is cast in gentler times.

But I will tell you an old woman's experience— that I can never remember a time, and that I do not know a work, which so requires to be rooted and grounded in God as ours.

You remember the question in the hymn, " Am I His, or am I not ? " IF I *am*, this is what is called our " hidden life with Christ in God." We all have a " hidden life " in ourselves, besides our outward working life. If our hidden life is filled with chatter and fancies, our outward working life will be the fruits of it.

" By their *fruits* ye shall know them," Christ says. Christ knows the good Nurse. It is not the good talker whom Christ knows as the good Nurse.

If our hidden life *is* " with Christ in God," by its fruits, too, it will be known.

What is it to live " with Christ in God " ? It is to live in Christ's spirit : forgiving any injuries, real or fancied, from our fellow-workers, from those above us as well as from those below (alas ! how small our injuries are that we should talk of forgiving !) thirsting after righteousness, righteous- ness, *i.e.* doing completely one's duty towards all with whom we have to do, towards God above as well as towards our fellow-nurses, our patients, our matron, home sister, and instructors ; fain to be holy as God is holy, perfect as our Father in Heaven is perfect in our hospital and training school ; caring for nothing more than for God's will in this His training ; careful for our sick and fellow-Nurses more than for ourselves ; active, like Christ, in our work ; like Christ, meek and lowly in heart in our Wards and " Home " ; peacemakers among our companions, which includes the never repeating anything which may do mischief ; placing our spirits in the Father's charge. ("I am the Almighty's charge," says the hymn.) *This* is to live a life with Christ in God.

You may have heard of Mr. Wilberforce. He it was who, after a long life of unremitting activity, varied only with disappointment, carried the Abolition of the Slave Trade, one of England's greatest titles to the gratitude of nations. Slavery, as Livingstone said, is the open sore of the world. (Mr. Clarkson and my grandfather were two of his fellow-workers.) Some one asked how Mr. Wilberforce did this, and a man I knew answered, " Because his life was hid with Christ in God."

Never was there a truer word spoken. And if we, when the time comes for us to be in charge of Wards, are enabled to "abolish" anything wrong in them, it can only be in the same way, by our life being hid with Christ in God. And no man or woman will do great things for God, or even small, whose "hidden life" is employed in self-complacency, or in thinking over petty slights, or of what other people are thinking of her.

We have three judges—our God, our neighbour, and ourselves. Our own judgment of ourselves is, perhaps, generally too favourable : our neighbour's judgment of us too unfavourable, except in the case of close friends, who may sometimes spoil each other. Shall we always remember to seek *God's* judgment of us, knowing this, that it will some day find us, whether we seek it or not ? *He* knows who is *His* nurse, and who is not.

This is laying the "foundation" ; *this* is the "hidden life with Christ in God" for us Nurses. "Keeping up to the mark," as St. Paul says ; and nothing else *will* keep us up to the mark in Nursing.

"Neglect nothing ; the most trivial action may be performed to ourselves, or performed to God."

What a pity that so many actions should be wasted by us Nurses in our Wards and in our "Home," when we might always be doing common things uncommonly well !

Small things *are* of consequence—small things are of *no* consequence ; we say this often to ourselves and to each other.

And both these sayings are true.

Every brick is of consequence, every dab of mortar, that it may be as good as possible in building up your house. A chain is no stronger than its weakest link : therefore every link is of consequence. And there can be no " small " thing in Nursing. How often we have seen a Nurse's life wrecked, in its usefulness, by some apparently small fault ! Perhaps this is to say that there can be no small things in the nursing service of God.

But in the service of ourselves, oh ! how small the things are ! Of no consequence indeed. How small they will appear to us all some day !

For what does it profit a Nurse if she gain the whole world to praise her, and lose her own soul in conceit ? What does it profit if the judgment of the whole world is for us Nurses, and God's is against us ?

It is a real danger, in works like these, when all men praise us. We must then see if we are " rooted and grounded in Christ Himself," to nurse as *He* would have us nurse, as *He* was in God, to do *His* Saviour-work. Am I His, or am I not?

It is a real danger, too, if in works like these we do not uphold the credit of our School. That is *not* bearing fruit. Can we hope, may we hope that, at least, some day, Christ may say even to our Training School, as He did once to His first followers, " Ye are the salt of the earth " ? But oh ! if we may hope this, let us never forget for one moment the terrible conclusion of that verse.

If we can, in the faintest sense, be called " the salt " of God's nursing world, let us watch, watch, watch, that we may never lose our " savour." One woman, as we well know, may be honoured by God to be " the salt " to purify a whole Ward. One woman may have lost her " savour," and a Ward be left without its " salt," and untold harm done.

We ought to be very much obliged to our kind Medical Instructor for the pains he has taken with us, and to show this by our careful attention. Without this there can be no improvement.

There is a time for all things—a time to be

trained, and a time to use our training. And if
we have thrown away the year we have here, we
can hardly recover it. Besides, what a shame it
is to come here, as Probationers, at considerable
cost (to others, most of us), and then not to make
our improvement the chief business of our lives,
so that at the end of our year we go away not
much better but rather worse than we came!
What account can we give of such a waste of
time and opportunities, of the best gifts of God,
to ourselves and to Him? " For God requireth
that which is past." If, when I was young,
there had been such opportunities of training for
Hospital work as you have, how eagerly I should
have made the most of them!

Therefore, " whatsoever thy hand findeth to
do, do it with all thy might " : be earnest in work,
be earnest also even in such things as taking
exercise and proper holiday. I say this particularly
to future Matrons and Sisters, for there should
be something of seriousness in keeping our bodies[1]
too up to the mark.

[1] Do you remember the word of one of the greatest poets of the Middle
Ages?
> The soul
> Which o'er the body keeps a holy ward,
> Placed there by God, yielding alone to Him
> *The trust He gave.*

H

Life is short, as preachers often tell us : that is,
each stage of it is apt to come to an end before
the work which belongs to it is finished.   Let us

> Act that each to-morrow
> Find us farther than to-day.

Let us be in earnest in work : above all,
because we believe this life to be the beginning of
another, into which we carry with us what we
have been and done here ; because we are working together with God (remember the Parting
Command !) and He is upholding us in our work
(remember the Parting Promise !) ; because, when
the hour of death approaches, we should wish to
think (like Christ) that we have completed life,
that we have finished the work which was given
us to do, that we have not lost one of those,
Patients or Nurses, who were entrusted to us.

What was the Parting Command ?   What was
the Parting Promise ?

We Nurses have just kept Ascension Day and
Whit-Sunday.   Shall we Nurses not remember the
Parting Command on Ascension Day—to preach
the Gospel to every creature ?   And the Parting
Promise : "And lo I am with you alway, even
unto the end of the world."

That Command and that Promise were given,

not to the Apostles or Disciples only, but to each and every one of us Nurses: to each to herself in her own Ward or Home.

Without the Promise the Command could not be obeyed. Without we obey the Command the Promise will not be fulfilled.

Christ tells us what He means by the Command. He tells us, over and over again: it is by ourselves, *by what we are in ourselves*, that we are " to preach the Gospel." *Not what we say, but what we do*, is the Preacher.   Not saying " Lord, Lord," —for how many ungodly things are done and said in the name of God—but " keeping his commandments," this it is which " preaches " Him ; it is the bearing much " fruit," not the saying many words. God's Spirit leads us rather to be silent than to speak, to do good works rather than to say fine things or to write them.

Over and over again, and especially in His first and last discourses, He insists upon this. He takes the sweet little child and places it in our midst : it was as if He had said " Ah ! that is the best preacher of you all." And those who have followed Him best have felt this most.

The most successful preacher the world has probably seen since St. Paul's time said, some 300 years ago, it was by *showing an example*, not by delivering a discourse, that the Apostles' work was really done, that the Gospel was really preached. And well did he show his own belief in this truth. For when all was ready for his mission to convert China to Christianity, and the plague broke out where he was, he stayed and nursed the plague.

We can, every one of us here present, though our teaching may not be much, by our *lives* "preach a continual sermon, that all who see may understand." (These words were found in the last letter, left unfinished, of a native convert of the "greatest missionary of modern times," Bishop Patteson, who was martyred in the South Sea Islands, in September 1871, and this convert with him. Oh, how he puts us to shame!)

It has happened to me — I daresay it has happened to every one of us—to be told by a Child-Patient, one who had been taught to say its prayers, that it "was afraid" to kneel down and "say its prayers" before a whole ward-full of people. Do we encourage and take care of such a little child? Shall we, when we have Wards under our own charge, take care that the Ward is kept so that none at proper times shall be "afraid" to kneel down and say their prayers? Do we reflect on the immense responsibility of a Nurse towards her helpless Sick, who depend upon her almost entirely for quiet, and thought, and order? Do we think that, as was once said, we are to no one as "rude" as we are to God?

I believe that one of our St. Thomas' Sisters, who is just leaving us after years of good work, is going to set up a "Home" for Sick Children, where, under her, they will be cared for in *all* ways. I am sure that we shall all bid her "God speed." And I know that many of those who have gone out from among us, and who are now Hospital Sisters or Nurses—they would not like me to mention their names—do care for their Patients, Children and all, in *all* ways. Thank God for it!

When a Patient, especially a child, sees you acting in all things as if in the presence of God— and none are so quick to observe it—then the names he or she heard at the Chaplain's or the Sister's or the Night Nurse's lips become names of real things and real Persons. There *is* a God, a Father; there *is* a Christ, a Comforter; there *is* a Spirit of Goodness, of Holiness; there *is* another world, to such an one.

When a Patient, especially a Child, sees us

acting as if there were *no* God, then there but too often becomes no God to him. Then words become to such a child mere words. And remember, that when such a Nurse—"salt" which has lost its "savour"—speaks to her Patients of God, she puts *a hindrance* in their way to keep them *from* God, instead of helping them *to* God. She had better not speak to them at all.

It is a terrible thought—I speak for myself—that we may *prevent* people from believing in God, instead of bringing them to "believe in God the Father Almighty."

What is it, "setting an example"? An example—*of what? Who* is *our* example, that we are to set? Christ is our example, our pattern : this we all know and say. And when this was once said—a very common word—before a very uncommon man, he said : "When you have your picture taken, the painter does not try to make it rather like, or not very unlike. It is not a good picture if it is not *exactly* like." Do we try to be *exactly* like Christ? If we do not, "are we His, or are we not?" Could it be said of each one of us : "That Nurse *is* (or is trying to be) exactly what Christ would have been in her place"?

Yet this is what every Nurse has to aim at.

Aim lower : and you cannot say then, " Christ is my example." Aim as high : and, after this life, " we shall be satisfied when we awake in His likeness."

But this aim cannot be carried out, it cannot even be entertained, without the Parting Promise. The Parting Promise was fulfilled to the disciples ten days afterwards, on Whit-Sunday, when the Holy Spirit was given them—that is, when Christ came as He promised, and was with them.

Christ comes to each Nurse of us all : and stands at our little room-door and knocks. Do we let Him in ?

The Holy Spirit comes, no more with outward show but with no less inward power, to each Ward and to each Nurse of us all, who is trying to do her Nursing and her Ward work *in God*, to live her hidden Nurse's life with Christ in God.

When your Patient asks you for a drink, you do not give him a stone. And shall not our Heavenly Father much more give His Spirit to each one of us, His nurses, when she asks Him? (*Are* we *His* nurses ?)

What is meant by the Spirit descending upon *us* Nurses, as it did on the first Whitsuntide? Is it not to put us in a state to nurse Him, by making our heart and our will His ? (He has really told us that nursing our Patients is nursing Him.) God asks the *heart* : that is, that we should consecrate *all* our self to Him—within as well as without, *within* even more than without—in doing the Nursing work He has given each one of us here to do.

Is it not to have the spirit of love, of courtesy, of justice, of right, of gentleness, of meekness, in our Training School ; the spirit of truth, of integrity, of energy and activity, of purity, which He *is*, in our Hospital? This it is to worship God in spirit and in truth. And we need not wait to go into a church, or even to kneel down at prayer, for *this* worship.

Is it not to feel that we desire really nothing for ourselves in our Nursing life, present and future, but only this, " Thy will be done," as we say in our daily prayer ? Is it not to trust Him, that *His will* is really the best for each one of us? How much there is in those two words, *His will*— the will of Almighty Wisdom and Goodness, which always *knows* what is best for each one of us Nurses, which always *wills* what is best, which always *can* do what it wills for our best.

Is it not to feel that the care and thought of

ourselves is lost in the thought of God and the care of our Patients and fellow-Nurses and Ward-Maids? Is it not to feel that we are never so happy as when we are working *with Him* and *for them*? And we Nurses can always do this, if we will.

Is not this what Christ meant when He said, "The kingdom of heaven is within you"? "The kingdom of heaven" consists not in much speaking but in doing, not in a sermon but in a heart. "The kingdom of heaven" can *always* be in a Nurse's blessed work, and even in her worries. Is not this what the Apostle meant when he told us to "rejoice in the Lord"? That is, to rejoice, whether Matrons, or Sisters, or Nurses, or Night Nurses, in the service of God (which, with us, means good Nursing of the Sick, good fellowship and high example as relates to our fellow-workers); to rejoice in the right, whoever does it; to rejoice in the truth, whoever has it; to rejoice in every good word and work, whoever it is; to rejoice, in one word, in what God rejoices in.

Let us thank God that some special aids to our spiritual life have been given us lately, for which I know many of us *are* thankful; and some of us have been able to keep this Whitsuntide as we never did before.

One little word more about our Training School. Training "consists in teaching people to bear responsibilities, and laying the responsibilities on them as they are able to bear them," as Bishop Patteson said of Education. The year which we spend here is generally the most important, as it may be the happiest, of our lives.

Here we find many different characters. Here we meet on a common stage, before we part company again to our several posts. If there are any rich among us, they are not esteemed for their riches. And the poor woman, the friendless, the lonely woman, receives a generous welcome. Every one who has any activity or sense of duty may qualify herself for a future useful life. Every one may receive situations without any reference, except to individual capacity, and to a kind of capacity which it is within the power of the most humble and unfriended to work out. Every one who has any natural kindness or courtesy in her, and who is not too much wrapped up in herself, may make pleasant friends.

Although we know how many and serious faults we have, ought we not also to be able to find here some virtues which do not equally flourish in the larger world ?—such as disinterested devotion to the calling we have chosen, and to which we can here fully give ourselves up without anxiety; warm-hearted interest in each other, for no one of us stands here in any other's way; freedom from jealousy and meanness; a generous self-denial in nursing our charges, and a generous sympathy with other Nurses; above all, an interest in our work, and an earnestness in taking the means given us to improve ourselves in what is to be so useful to others.

And this is also the surest sign of our improvement in it. This is what St. Paul calls: "Not slothful in business, fervent in spirit, serving the Lord."

Always, however, we must be above our work and our worries, keeping our souls free in that "hidden life" of which it has been spoken.

Above all, let us pray that God will send real workers into this immense "field" of Nursing, made more immense this year by the opening out of London *District* Nursing at the bedside of the sick poor at home. A woman who takes a sentimental view of Nursing (which she calls "ministering," as if she were an angel), is of course worse than useless. A woman possessed with the idea that she is making a sacrifice will never do ; and a woman who thinks any kind of Nursing work " beneath a Nurse " will simply be in the way. But if the right woman is moved by God to come to us, what a welcome we will give her, and how happy she will soon be in a work, the many blessings of which none can know as we know them, though we know the worries too ! (Good Bishop Patteson used to talk to his assistants something in this way ; would we were like him !)

Nurses' work means downright work, in a cheery, happy, hopeful, friendly spirit. An earnest, bright, cheerful woman, without that notion of " making sacrifices," etc., perpetually occurring to her mind, is the real Nurse. Soldiers are sent anywhere, and leave home and country for years ; *they* think nothing of it, because they go " on duty." Shall *we* have less self-denial than they, and think less of " duty " than these men ? A woman with a healthy, active tone of mind, plenty of work in her, and some enthusiasm, who makes the best of everything, and, above all, does not think herself better than other people because she is a " Nightingale Nurse," that is the woman we want.

(Must I tell you again, what I have had to tell you before, that we have a great name in the world for—conceit?)

I suppose, of course, that sound religious principle is at the bottom of her.

Now, if there be any young persons really in earnest whom any of you could wish to see engaged in this work, if you know of any such, and feel justified in writing to them, you will be aiding materially in this work if you will put it in their power to propose themselves as Candidates.

My every-day thought is—" How will God provide for the introduction of real Christianity among all of us Nurses, and among our Patients?" My every-day prayer (and I know that the prayer of many of you is the same) is that He will give us the means and show us how to use them, and give us the people. We ask you to pray for us, who have to arrange for you, as we pray for you, who have to nurse the Patients; and I know you do. The very vastness of the work raises one's thoughts to God, as the only One by whom it can be done. That is the solid comfort—*He knows*. He loves us all, and our Patients infinitely more than we can. He is, we trust, sending us to them; He will bless honest endeavours to do

His work among them. Without *this* belief and support, it seems to me, when we look at the greatness of the work, and how far, far we fall short of it, instead of being conceited, we should not have courage to work at all.

And when we say the words in the Communion Service—"Therefore with angels and archangels," do we think whether we are fit company for angels? It may not be fanciful to believe that "angels and archangels," to whom all must seem so different, may see God's light breaking over the Nursing Service, though perhaps in our time it may not attain the perfect day. Only we must work on, and bring no hindrances to that light. And that not one of us may bring hindrances to that light, believe me, let us pray daily.

I have been longer than I intended or hoped, and will only say one more word.

May we each and all of us Nurses be faithful to the end, remembering this, that no one Nurse stands alone. May we not say, in the words of the prophet, that it is "The Lord" who "hath gathered" us Nurses "together out of the lands"? "It is because we do not *praise* as we proceed," said a good and great man, " that our progress is so slow." Should not all this Training School be so melted into one heart and mind, that we may with *one* heart and mind act and nurse and sing together our praise and thanksgiving, blessing and gratitude, for mercies, every one of which seems to belong to the whole School ? For every Nurse alike belongs to the Mother School of which she is a part, and to the Almighty Father, who has sent her here, and to whom alone we each and all of us Nurses owe everything we have and are.

F. N.

V

April 28, 1876.

MY DEAR FRIENDS,—Again another year has brought us together to rejoice at our successes, and, if to grieve over some disappointments, to try together to find out what it is that may have brought them about, and to correct it.

God seems to have given His favour to the manner in which you have been working.

Thanks to you, each and all of you, for the pains you have taken to carry out the work. I hope you feel how great have been the pains bestowed upon you.

You are not " grumblers " at all : you do try to justify the great care given you, the confidence placed in you, and, after you have left this Home, the freedom of action you enjoy—by that *intelligent* obedience to rules and orders, to render which is alone worthy of the name of " Trained Nurse," of God's soldier. We shall be poor soldiers indeed, if we don't *train* ourselves for the battle. But if discipline is ever looked upon as interference, then freedom has become lawlessness, and we are no " Trained Nurses " at all.

The trained Englishwoman is the first Nurse in the world : *if*—IF she knows how to unite this intelligent obedience to commands with thoughtful and godly command of herself.

" The greatest evils in life," said one of the world's highest statesmen, " have had their rise from something which was thought of too little importance to attend to." How we Nurses can echo that !

" Immense, incalculable misery " is due to " the immoral thoughtlessness "—he calls thoughtlessness immoral—of women about little things. This is what our training is to counteract in us. Think nothing too small to be attended to in this way. Think everything too small of personal trouble or sensitiveness to be cared for in another way.

It is not knowledge only : it is practice we want. We only *know* a thing if we can *do* it. There is a famous Italian proverb which says : " So much "—and no more—" each knows as she does."

I

What we did last year we may look upon not as a matter of conceit, but of encouragement. We must not fail this year, and we'll not fail. We'll keep up to the mark : nay more, we will press on to a higher mark. For our " calling " is a high one (the " little things," remember : a high excellence in little things). And we must answer to the call ever more and more strenuously and ever more and more humbly too.

We live together : let us live for each other's comfort. We are all working together : grasp the idea of this as a larger work than our own little pet hobbies, which are very narrow, our own little personal wishes, feelings, piques, or tempers. This is not individual work. A real Nurse sinks self. Remember we are not so many small selves, but members of a community.

" Little children, love one another." To love, that is, to help one another, to strive together, to act together, to work for the same end, to bring to perfection the sisterly feeling of fellow-workers, without which nothing great is done, nothing good lasts. Might not St. John have been thinking of us Nurses in our Training Schools when he said that ?

May God be with us all and we be *one* in Him
and in His *work* !

God speed us all !
Amen in our hearts.

I

These are some of the little things we need to
attend to :

To be a Nurse *is* to be a Nurse : not to be a
Nurse only when we are put to the work we like.
If we can't work when we are put to the work we
don't like—and Patients can't always be fitted to
Nurses—that is behaving like a spoilt child, like a
naughty girl : not like a Nurse.

If we can do the work we don't like from the
higher motive till we do like it, that is one test of
being a real Nurse. A Nurse is not one who can
only do what she does like, and can't do what she
does not like. For the Patients want according to
their wants, and not according to the Nurse's likes
or dislikes.

If you wish to be trained to do *all* Nursing
well, even what you do not like—trained to perfection in little things—that is Nursing for the
sake of Nursing, for the sake of God and of your

neighbour. And remember, in little things as in great—No Cross, no Crown.

Nursing is said, most truly said, to be a high calling, an honourable calling.

But what does the honour lie in ? In working hard during your training to learn and to do all things perfectly. The honour does not lie in putting on Nursing like your uniform, your dress ; though dishonour often lies in being neat in your uniform within doors and dressy in your finery out of doors. Dishonour always lies in inconsistency.

Honour lies in loving perfection, consistency, and in working hard for it : in being ready to work patiently : ready to say not " How clever I am ! " but " I am not yet worthy : but Nursing is worthy ; and I will live to deserve and work to deserve to be called a Trained Nurse."

Here are two of the plain, practical, little things necessary to produce good Nurses, the want of attention to which produces some of the " greatest evils in life" : quietness, cleanliness. (a) Quietness in moving about the " Home " ; in arranging your rooms, in not *slamming* every door after you. No noisy talking on the stairs and in the lobbies— forgetting at times some unfortunate Night Nurse in bed. But if you are Nurses, Nurses ought to be going about quietly whether Night Nurses are asleep or not. For a Sick Ward ought to be as quiet as a Sick Room ; and a Sick Room, I need not say, ought to be the quietest place in God's Kingdom. Quietness in dress, especially being *consistent* in this matter when off duty and going out. And oh ! let the Lady Probationers realise how important their example is in these things, so little and so great ! If you are Nurses, Nurses ought not to be dressy, whether in or out of their uniform.

Do you remember that Christ holds up the wild flowers as our example in dress? Why? He says : God " clothes " the field flowers. How does He clothe them?

First : their " clothes " are exactly suitable for the kind of place they are in and the kind of work they have to do. So should ours be.

Second : field flowers are never double : double flowers change their useful stamens for showy petals, and so have no seeds. These double flowers are like the useless appendages now worn on the dress, and very much in your way. Wild flowers have purpose in all their beauty. So ought dress to have ; nothing purposeless about it.

Third : the colours of the wild flower are perfect in harmony, and not many of them.

Fourth : there is not a speck on the freshness with which flowers come out of the dirty earth. Even when our clothes are getting rather old we may imitate the flower : for we may make them look as fresh as a daisy.

Whatsoever we do, whether we eat or drink *or dress*, let us do all to the glory of God. But above all remember, " Be not anxious what ye shall put on," which is the real meaning of " Take no thought."

This is not my own idea : it was in a Bible lesson, never to be forgotten. And I knew a Nurse who dressed so nicely and quietly after she had heard this Bible lesson that you would think of her as a model. And alas ! I have known, oh how many ! whose dress was their snare.

Oh, my dear Nurses, whether gentlewomen or not, don't let people say of you that you are like " Girls of the Period " : let them say that you are like " field flowers," and welcome.

(*b*) Cleanliness in person and in our rooms, thinking nothing too small to be attended to in this respect. And if these things are important in the " Home," think how important they are in the Wards, where cleanliness and fresh air—there can be no pure air without cleanliness—not so much give life as *are* the very life of the Patients ; where the smallest carelessness may turn the scale from life to death ; where Disinfectants, as one of your own Surgeons has said, are but a " mystic rite." Cleanliness is the only real Disinfectant. Remember that Typhoid Fever is distinctly a filth disease ; that Consumption is distinctly the product of breathing foul air, especially at night ; that in surgical cases, Erysipelas and Pyaemia are simply a poisoning of the blood—generally thro' some want of cleanliness or other. And do not speak of these as little things, which determine the most momentous issues of life and death. I knew a Probationer who when washing a poor man's ulcerated leg, actually wiped it on his sheet, and excused herself by saying she had always seen it done so in another place. The least carelessness in not washing your hands between one bad case and another, and many another carelessness which it is plain I cannot mention here—it would not be nice, though it is much less nice to do it —the least carelessness, I say, in these things which every Nurse can be careful or careless in, may cost a life : aye, may cost your own, or at least a finger. We have all seen poisoned fingers.

I read with more interest than if they were novels your case papers. Some are meagre, especially in the "history." Some are good. Please remember that, besides your own instruction, you can give me some too, by making these most interesting cases as interesting as possible, by making them full and accurate, and entering the full history. If the history of every case were recorded, especially of Typhoid Fever, which is, as we said, a filth disease, it is impossible to over-estimate the body of valuable information which would thus be got together, and might go far, in the hands of Officers of Health and by recent laws, to prevent disease altogether. The District Nurses are most useful in this respect.

When we obey all God's laws as to cleanliness, fresh air, pure water, good habits, good dwellings, good drains, food and drink, work and exercise, health is the result. When we disobey, sickness. 110,000 lives are needlessly sacrificed every year in this kingdom by our disobedience, and 220,000 people are needlessly sick all the year round. And why? Because we will not know, will not obey God's simple Health laws.

No epidemic can resist thorough cleanliness and fresh air.

Is there any Nurse here who is a Pharisee? This seems a very cruel and unjust question.

We think of the Pharisees, when we read the terrible denunciation of them by our Master, as a small, peculiar, antiquated sect of 2000 years ago. Are they not rather the least peculiar, the most widely-spread people of every time? I am sure I often ask myself, sadly enough, "Am I a Pharisee?" In this sense: Am I, or am I not, doing this with a single eye to God's work, to serving Him and my neighbour, even tho' my "neighbour" is as hostile to me as the Jew was to the Samaritan? Or am I doing it because I identify my selfish self with the work, and in so doing serve myself and not God? If so, then I am a Pharisee.

It is good to love our Training School and our body, and to wish to keep up its credit. We are bound to do so. That is helping God's work in the world. We are bound to try to be the " salt of the world " in nursing ; but if we are conceited, seeking *ourselves* in this, then we are not " salt " but Pharisees.

We should have zeal for God's sake and His work's sake : but some seem to have zeal for zeal's sake only. Zeal does not make a Christian Nurse if it is zeal for our own credit and glory —tho' Christ was the most zealous mediciner that ever was. (He says : " The zeal of God's house hath eaten me up.") Zeal by itself does not make a good Nurse : it makes a Pharisee. Christ is so strong upon this point of not being conceited, of not nursing to show what " fine fellows " we are as Nurses, that He actually says " it is conceited of us to let one of our hands know what the other does." What will He say if He sees one of us doing all her work to let not only her other hand but other people know she does it? Yet all our best work which looks so well *may* be done from this motive.

And let me tell you a little secret. One of our Superintendents at a distance says that she finds she must not boast so much about St. Thomas'. Nor must you. People have heard too much about it. I dare say you remember the fine old Greek statesman who was banished because people were tired of hearing him called " The Just." Don't let people get tired of hearing you call St. Thomas' " The Just " when you are away from us. We shall not at all complain of your proving it "The Just" by your training and conduct.

I read lately in a well-known medical journal, speaking of the "Nightingale Nurses," that the day is quite gone by when a novel would give a caricature of a Nurse as a "Mrs. Gamp"—drinking, brutal, ignorant, coarse old woman. The "Nightingale Nurse" in a novel, it said, would be—what do you think?—an active, useful, clever Nurse. These are the parts I approve of. But what else do you think?—a lively, rather pert, and very conceited young woman. Ah, there's the rub. You see what our name is "up" for in the world. That's what I should like to be left out. This is what a friendly critic says of us, and we may be very sure that unfriendly critics say much worse. Do we deserve what they say of us? That is the question. Let us not have, each one of us, to say "yes" in our own hearts. Christ made no light matter of conceit.

Keep the usefulness, and let the conceit go.

And may I here say a few words of counsel to those who may be called upon to be Night Nurses? One of these asked me with tears to pray for her.

I do pray for all of you, our dear Night Nurses. In my restless nights my thoughts turn to you incessantly by the bedsides of restless and suffering Patients, and I pray God that He will make, thro' you, thro' your patience, your skill, your hope, faith and charity, every Ward into a Church, and teach us that to *be* the Gospel is the only way to " preach the Gospel," which Christ tells us is the duty of every one of us " unto the end of the world "—every woman and Nurse of us all ; and that a collection of any people trying to live like Christ is a Church. Did you ever think how Christ was a Nurse, and stood by the bed, and with His own hands nursed and " did for " the sufferers ?

But, to return to those who may be called upon to be Night Nurses : do not abuse the liberty given you on emerging from the " Home," where you are cared for as if you were our children. Keep to regular hours by day for your meals, your sleep, your exercise. If you do not, you will never be able to do and stand the night work perfectly ; if you do, there is no reason why night nursing may not be as healthy as day. (I used to be very fond of the night when I was a Night Nurse ; I know what it is. But then I had my day work to do besides ; you have not.) Do not turn dressy in your goings out by day. It is vulgar, it is mean, to burst out into freedom in this way. There are circumstances of peculiar temptation when, after the restraint and motherly care of the " Home," you, the young ones, are put into circumstances of peculiar liberty. Is it not the time to act like Daniel ? . . . Let " the Judge, the Righteous Judge," have to call us not the " Pharisees," but Daniel's band !

That is what I pray for you, for me, for all of us.

But what is it to be a Daniel's band? What is God's command to Night Nurses? It is—is it not ?—not to slur over any duty—not the very least of all our duties—as Night Nurse : to be able to give a full, accurate, and minute account of each Patient the next morning : to be strictly reserved in your manner with gentlemen ("Thou God seest me " : no one else) ; to be honest and true. You don't know how well the Patients know you, how accurately they judge you. You can do them no good unless they see that you *live* what you say.

It is : not to go out showily dressed, and not to keep irregular hours with others in the day time.

> Dare to have a purpose firm,
> Dare to make it known.

Watch—watch. Christ seems to have had a

special word for Night Nurses : " I say unto you,
watch." And He says : " Lo, I am with you
alway," when no one else is by.

And he divides us all, at this moment, into the
" wise virgins " and the " foolish virgins." Oh, let
Him not find any " foolish virgins " among our
Night Nurses ! Each Night Nurse has to stand
alone in her Ward.

Dare to stand alone.

Let our Master be able to say some day that
every one of the Patients has been the better, not
only in body but in spirit—whether going to life
or to death—for having been nursed by each one
of you.

But one is gone, perhaps the dearest of all—
Nurse Martha Rice.

I was the last to see her in England. She was
so pleased to be going to Miss Machin at Montreal.
She said it was no sacrifice, except the leaving her
parents. She almost wished it had been, that she
might have had something to give to God.

Now she *has* had something to give to God :
her life.

" So young, so happy : all so happy together,

when in their room they were always sitting round the table, so cheerful, reading their Bible together. She walked round the garden so happy that last night."

So pure and fresh : there was something of the sweet savour of holiness about her. I could tell you of souls upon whom she made a great impression : all unknowing : simply by being herself.

A noble sort of girl : sound and holy in mind and heart : living with God. It is scarcely respectful to say how I liked her, now she is an angel in heaven ; like a child to Miss Machin, who was like a mother to her, loved and nursed her day and night.

"So dear and bright a creature," "liked and respected by every one in the Hospital," " and, as a Nurse, hardly too much can be said in her favour." " To the Doctors, Patients, and Superintendent, she was simply invaluable." " The contrast between these Nurses and the best of others is to be keenly felt daily " ; " doing bravely " ; " perfectly obedient and pleasant to their Superintendent."

Was Martha conceited with all this ? She was one of the simplest humblest Christian women I have ever known. All noble souls are simple, natural, and humble.

Let us be like her, and, like her, not conceited with it all. She was too brave to be conceited : too brave not to be humble. *She* had trained herself for the battle.

"With a nice, genial, respectful manner, which never left her, great firmness in duty, and steadiness that rendered her above suspicion " : " happy and interested in her charge."

More above all petty calculations about self, all paltry wranglings, than almost any. How different for us, for her, had it not been so ! Could we have mourned her as we do ? The others of the small Montreal staff who miss her so terribly will like to hear how we feel this. They were all with her when she died. Miss Machin sat up with her every night, and either she or Miss Blower never left her, day or night, during the last nine days of her illness. She died of typhoid fever : peritonitis the last three weeks ; but, as she had survived so long, they hoped against hope up to Easter Day.

About seven days before her death, during her delirium, she said : " The Lord has two wills : His will be done." It is when we do not know what God's will is to be, that it is the hardest to will what He wills.

Strange to say, on Good Friday, though she was

so delirious that there was difficulty in keeping her in bed, and she did not know what day it was, Christ on the Cross was her theme all the day long. " Christ died on the Cross for me, and I want to go and die for Him." She had indeed lived for Him. Then on Easter Day she said to Miss Blower : " I am happy, so happy : we are both happy, so very happy." She said she was going to hear the eighth Psalm. Shall we remember Martha's favourite psalm ? She spoke often about St. Thomas'.

She died the day after Easter Day. The change came at 7 in the evening, and she lived till 5 o'clock the next morning, conscious to the last, repeating sentences, and answering by looks when she could speak no more. Her Saviour, whom she had so loved and followed in her life, was with her thro' the Valley of the Shadow of Death, and she felt Him there. She was happy. " My best love," she said, " tell them it is all for the best, and I am not sorry I came out."

Her parents have given her up nobly, though with bleeding hearts, with true submission to our Father's will : they *are* satisfied it is " all for the best."

All the Montreal Hospital shared our sorrow. The Doctors were full of kindness in their medical

attendance.   Mr. Redpath, who is a principal
Director, and Mrs. Redpath were like a real father
and mother to our people.   Martha's death-bed
and coffin were strewed with flowers.

Public and private prayers were offered up for
her at Montreal during her illness.   Who can say
that they were not answered?

She spoke of dying : but without fear.   We
prayed that God would spare the child to us : but
He had need of her.

Our Father arranged her going out : for she
went, if ever woman did, with a single eye to please
Him and do her duty to the work and her Superintendent.   "Is it well with the child ? "   " It is
well."   Let us who feel her loss so deeply in the
work not grudge her to God.

As one of you yourselves said : "She died like
a good soldier of Jesus Christ, well to the front."
Would any one of us wish it otherwise for her ?
Would any one of us wish a better lot for herself ?
There is but one feeling among us all about her :
that she lived as a noble Christian girl, and that
she has been permitted to die nobly : in the post
of honour, as a soldier thinks it glorious to die.
In the midst of our work, so surely do we Nurses
think it glorious to die.

But to be like her we must have a mind like hers : " enduring, patient, firm, and meek." I know that she sought of God the mind of Jesus Christ, " active, like His ; like His, resigned " ; copying His pattern : ready to " endure hardness."

We give her joy ; it is our loss, not hers. She is gone to our Lord and her Lord, made ripe so soon for her and our Father's house. Our tears are her joy. She is in another room of our Father's house. She bids us now give thanks for her. Think of that Easter morn when she rose again ! She had indeed " another morn than ours "—that 17th of April.

FLORENCE NIGHTINGALE.

VI

My dear Friends,—I am always thinking of you, and as my Easter greeting, I could not help copying for you part of a letter which one of my brother-in-law's family had from Col. Degacher (commanding one battalion of the 24th Regiment in Natal), giving the names of men whom he recommended for the Victoria Cross, when defending the Commissariat Stores at Rorke's Drift. (His brother, Capt. Degacher, was killed at Isandhlwana.) He says:

"Private John Williams was posted, together with Private Joseph Williams and Private William Harrison (1/24th Regiment), in a further ward of the Hospital. They held it for more than an hour—so long as they had a round of ammunition left, when, as communication was for the time cut off, the Zulus were enabled to advance and burst open the door. A hand-to-hand conflict then ensued, during which Private Joseph Williams and two of the Patients were dragged out and assegaied (killed with a short spear or dagger).

"Whilst the Zulus were occupied with the slaughter of these unfortunate men, a lull took place, which enabled Private John Williams (who with two of the Patients were by this time the *only men left alive* in the Ward) to succeed in knocking a hole in the partition and taking the two Patients with him into the next ward, where he found Private Henry Hook.

"These two men together, one man working whilst the other fought and held the enemy at bay with his bayonet, broke through three more partitions, and were thus enabled to bring eight Patients through a small window into the inner line of defence.

"In another ward facing the hill, William Jones and Private Robert Jones had been placed: they defended their post to the last, and until six out of seven Patients it contained had been removed. The seventh, Sergeant Maxfield, 2/24th Regiment, was delirious from fever, and although they had previously dressed him, they were unable to induce him to move; and when Private Robert Jones returned to endeavour to carry him off, he found him being stabbed on his bed by the Zulus.

"Corporal Wm. Allen and Fd. Hitch, 2/24th Regiment, must also be mentioned. It was chiefly due to their courageous conduct that communication with the Hospital was kept up at all—holding together, at all costs, a most dangerous post, raked in reverse by the enemy's fire from the hill. They were both severely wounded, but their determined conduct enabled the Patients to be withdrawn from the Hospital. And when incapacitated from their wounds from fighting themselves, they continued, as soon as their wounds were dressed, to serve out ammunition to their comrades throughout the night."

These men who were defending the house at Rorke's Drift were 120 of his (Col. Degacher's) men against 5000 Zulus, and they fought from 3 P.M. of January 22nd, to 5 A.M. of the 23rd. *There* is a Night Nurse's work for you. "When shall such heroes live again?" In every Nurse of us all. Every Nurse may at all costs serve her Patients as these brave heroic men did at the risk and the cost of their own lives.

Three cheers for these bravest of Night Nurses of Rorke's Drift, who regarded not themselves,

not their ease, not even their lives ; who regarded
duty and discipline ; who stood to the last by
God and their neighbour ; who saved their post
and their Patients. And may we Nurses all be
like them, and fight through the night for our
Patients' lives — fight through every night and
day !

Do you see what a high feeling of comradeship
does for these men ?   Many a soldier loses his life
in the field by going back to help a drowning or
a wounded comrade, who might have saved it.
Oh, let us Nurses all be *comrades* ; stick to the
honour of our flag and our corps, and help each
other to the best success, for the sake of Him
who died, as at this time, to save us all !

And let us remember that petty selfishnesses
and meannesses and self-indulgences hinder our
honour as good soldiers of Jesus Christ and of the
Unseen God, who sees all these little things when
no one else does !

What makes us endure to the end ?   Discipline.
Do you think these men could thus have fought
at a desperate post through the livelong night if
they had not been trained to obedience to orders,
and to acting as a corps, yet each man doing his
own duty to the fullest extent—rather than every

man going his own way, thinking of his own likings, and caring for himself?

How *great* may be men and women, "little lower than the angels," and also how *little*!

Humility—to think our own life worth nothing except as serving in a corps, God's nursing corps, unflinching obedience, steadiness, and endurance in carrying out His work—that is true discipline, that is true greatness, and may God give it to us Nurses, and make us His own Nurses.

And let us not think that these things can be done in a day or a night. No, they are the result of no rough-and-ready method. The most important part of those efforts was to be found in the patient labour of years. These great tasks are not to be accomplished suddenly by raw fellows in a night; it is when discipline and training have become a kind of second nature to us that they can be accomplished every day and every night. The raw Native levies ran away, determining our fall at Isandhlwana. The well-trained English soldiers, led by their Officers and their Non-commissioned Officers, stuck to their posts.

Every feeling, every thought we have, stamps a character upon us, especially in our year of training, and in the next year or two.

The most unruly boys, weak in themselves—for unruliness is weakness—when they have to submit, it brings out all the good points in their characters. These boys, so easily led astray, they put themselves under the severest discipline, and after training sometimes come out the best of us all. The qualities which, when let alone, run to seed and do themselves and others nothing but harm, under proper discipline make fine fellows of them.

And what is it to obey? To obey means to do what we are told, and to do it at once. With the nurse, as with the soldier, whether we have been accustomed to it or not, whether we think it right or not, is not the question. Prompt obedience is the question. We are not in control, but under control. Prompt obedience is the first thing; the rest is traditional nonsense. But mind who we go to for our orders. Go to headquarters. True discipline is to uphold authority, and not to mind trouble. We come into the work to do the work. . . .

We Nurses are taught the "reason why," as soldiers cannot be, of much of what we have to do. But it would be making a poor use of this "reason why" if we were to turn round in any

part of our training and say, or *not* say, but *feel*—
We know better than you.

Would we be of less use than the Elephant?
The Elephant who could kill a hundred men, but
who alike pushes the artillery train with his head
when the horses cannot move it, and who minds
the children and carefully nurses them, and who
threads a needle with his trunk. Why? Because
he has been taught to *obey*. He would be of no
use but to destroy, unless he had learnt that.
Sometimes he has a strong will, and it is not easy
for him to get his lesson perfect. We can feel
for him. We know a little about it ourselves.
But he does learn in time to go our way and not
his own, to carry a heavy load, which of course
he would rather not do, to turn to which ever side
we wish, and to stop when we want him to stop.

So God teaches each one of us in time to go
His way and not our own. And one of the best
things I can wish each one of us is that we may
learn the Elephant's lesson, that is to obey, in
good time and not too late.

Pray for me, my dear friends, that I may learn
it, even in my old age.

FLORENCE NIGHTINGALE.

VII

My dear Friends,—Here, one year more, is my very best love and heart-felt " good speed " to the work.

To each and to all I wish the very highest success, in the widest meaning of the word, in the life's work you have chosen.

And I am more sorry than for anything else that my illness, more than usually serious, has let me know personally so little of you, except through our dear Matron and dear Home Sister.

You are going steadily and devotedly on in preparing yourselves for future work. Accept my heartiest sympathy and thanks.

We hear much of " Associations " now. It is impossible indeed to live in isolation : we are dependent upon others for the supply of all our wants, and others upon us.

Every Hospital is an " Association " in itself.

We of this School are an Association in the deepest sense, regulated—at least we strive towards it—on high and generous principles ; through organisation working at once for our own and our fellow Nurses' success. For, to make progress possible, we must make this interdependence a source of good : not a means of standing still.

There is no magic in the word "Association," but there is a secret, a mighty call in it, *if* we will but listen to the "still small voice" in it, calling upon each of us to do our best.

It calls upon our dear heads, and they answer. It calls upon each of us.

We must never forget that the "Individual" makes the Association. What the Association *is* depends upon each of its members. A Nurses' Association can never be a substitute for the individual Nurse. It is she who must, each in her measure, give life to the Association, while the Association helps *her*.

We *have* our dear heads. Thank God for them ! Let us each one of us be a living member, according to her several ability. It is the individual that signifies—rather than the law or the rule.

Has not every one who has experience of the world been struck by this : you may have the most admirable circumstances and organisations and examinations and certificates, yet, if the individual allows herself to sink to a lower level, it is all but a "tinkling cymbal" for her. It is how the circumstances are worked that signifies. Circumstances are opportunities.

Rules may become a dead letter. It is the spirit of them that "giveth life." It is the individual, inside, that counts, the level she is upon which tells. The rest is only the outward shell or envelope. She must become a "rule of thought" to herself through the Ruler.

And on the other hand, it strikes you often, as a great man has said, if the individual finds herself afterwards in less admirable circumstances, but keeps her high level, and rises to a higher and a higher level still—if she makes of her difficulties, her opportunities—steps to ascend—she commands her circumstances; she is capable of the best Nursing work and spirit, capable of the best influence over her Patients.

It is again, what the individual Nurse *is* and can do during her *living* training and *living* work that signifies, not what she is certified for, like a steam-boiler, which is certified to stand so much pressure of work.

She may have gone through a first-rate course, plenty of examinations, and we may find nothing inside. It may be the difference between a Nurse nursing, and a Nurse reading a book on Nursing. Unless it bear fruit, it is all gilding and veneering: the reality is not there, growing, growing every year. Every Nurse must grow. No Nurse can stand still. She must go forward or she will go backward every year.

And how can a Certificate or public Register show this? Rather, she ought to have a moral "Clinical" Thermometer in herself. Our stature does not grow every year after we are "grown up." Neither does it grow down. It is otherwise with our moral stature and our Nursing stature. We grow down, if we don't grow up, every year.

At the present time, when there are so many Associations, when periodicals and publicity are so much the fashion, when there is such a dragging of everything before the public, there is some danger of our forgetting that any true Nursing work must be quiet work—an individual work. Anything else is contrary to the whole realness of the work. *Where* am *I*, the individual, in my inmost soul? *What* am *I*, the inner woman called "I"? That is the question.

This "I" must be quiet yet quick; quick without hurry; gentle without slowness, discreet without self-importance. "In quietness and in confidence must be her strength."

I must be trustworthy, to carry out directions intelligently and perfectly, *unseen* as well as seen; "unto the Lord" *as well as* unto men; no mere eye service. (How can this be if she is a mere Association Nurse, and not an individual Nurse?)

I must have moral influence over my Patients. And I *can* only have this by *being* what I appear, especially now that everybody is educated, so that Patients become my keen critics and judges. My Patients are watching me. They know what my profession, my calling is: to devote myself to the good of the sick. They are asking themselves: does that Nurse act up to her profession? This is no supposition. It is a fact. It is a call to us, to each individual Nurse, to act up to her profession.

We hear a good deal nowadays about Nursing being made a "profession." Rather, is it not the question for *me*: *am I* living up to my "profession"?

But I must not crave for the Patient to be always recognising my services. On the contrary:

the best service I can give is that the Patient shall scarcely be aware of any—shall recognise my presence most by recognising that he has *no* wants.

(Shakespeare tells me that to be " nurse like " is to be to the Patient—

> So kind, so duteous, diligent,
> So tender over his occasions, true,
> So feat.)

I must be thorough—a work, not a word—a Nurse, not a book, not an answer, not a certificate, not a mechanism, a mere piece of a mechanism or Association.

At the same time, in as far as Associations really give help and pledges for progress, are not mere crutches, stereotypes for standing still, let us bid them " God speed " with our whole hearts.

We all know what " parasites " are, plants or animals which live upon others and don't work for their own food, and so degenerate. For the work to get food is quite as necessary as the food itself for healthy active life and development.

Now, there is a danger in the air of becoming Parasites in Nursing (and also Midwifery)—of our becoming Nurses (and Midwives) by deputy, a danger now when there is so great an inclination to make school and college education, all sorts of

Sciences and Arts, even Nursing and Midwifery, a book and examination business, a profession in the low, not in the high sense of the word. And the danger is that we shall be content to let the book and the theory and the words do for us. One of the most religious of men says that we let the going to Church and the clergyman do for us *instead of* the learning and the practice, if we have the Parasite tendency, and that even the better the service and the better the sermon and the theory and the teaching, the more danger there is that we may let it do. He says that we may become satisfied to be prayed for instead of praying—to have our work for Christ done by a paid deputy—to be fed by a deputy who gives us our supply for a week—to substitute for thought what is meant as a stimulus to thought and practice. This is the parasite of the pew he says (as the literary parasite thinks he knows everything because he has a "good library"). He enjoys his weekly, perhaps his daily worship, while character and life, will and practice are not only not making progress, but are actually deteriorating.

Do you remember Tennyson's farmer, who says of the clergyman :

I 'eärd 'um a bummin' awaäy . . . ower my 'eäd, . . .
An' I thowt a said whot a owt to 'a said an' I coom'd awaäy.

We laugh at that. But is the Parasite much better than that?

Now the Ambulance Classes, the Registration, the Certificates of Nursing and of Nurses (and of midwifery), especially any which may demand the minimum of *practice*, which may *substitute* for *personal* progress in active proficiency, mere literary or word progress, instead of making it the material for growth in correct knowledge and practice, all such like things may tend this way.

It is not the certificate which makes the Nurse or the Midwife. It may *un-make* her. The danger is lest she let the certificate be *instead of* herself, *instead of* her own never ceasing going up higher as a woman and a Nurse.

This is the "day" of Examinations in the turn that Education—Elementary, the Higher Education, Professional Education—seems taking. And it is a great step which has substituted this for what used to be called "interest." Only let us never allow it to encroach upon what cannot be tested by examinations. Only let the "day" of *Practice*, the development of each individual's thought and practice, character and dutifulness, keep up, through the materials given us for growth and for correct knowledge, with the "day of examinations" in the Nurse's life, which is above all a moral and practical life, a life not of show, but of faithful action.

But above all, dear comrades, let each one of us, each individual of us, not only bid "God speed" in her heart to this, our own School (or Association—call it so if you will), but *strive* to *speed* it with all the best that is in her, even as your "Association" and its dear heads strive to speed each one of you.

Let each one of us take the abundant and excellent food for the mind which is offered us, in our training, our classes, our lectures, our examinations and reading — not as "Parasites," no, none of you will ever do that—but as bright and vigorous fellow - workers, working out the better way every day to the end of life.

Once more, my heartiest sympathy, my dearest love to each and to all of you,

from your ever faithful old comrade,

FLORENCE NIGHTINGALE.

Printed by R. & R. CLARK, LIMITED, *Edinburgh*.

And don't despise what
some of you call 'housemaid's
work.' If you thought of
its extreme importance, you
would not mind doing it.
As you know, without thorough
housemaid's work, every thing
in the Ward or Sick room
becomes permeated with
organic matter

The greatest Compliment I
ever thought I, as a Hospital nurse,
received was: that I was put
to clean & "do" the Special Ward,
with the severest Medical or
Surgical case which I was
nursing, every day: because I
did it thoroughly & without
disturbing the Patient

THE LIFE OF
FLORENCE NIGHTINGALE

BY

SIR EDWARD COOK

With Portraits. 2 Vols. 8vo. 30s. net.

DAILY CHRONICLE.—"A book of surpassing charm, worthy of the theme; in fine, a great biography of a great woman. We have no hesitation in saying that this book will live as one of the greatest biographies in the English language."

MORNING POST.—"One of the most remarkable books of our time. For Sir Edward Cook has made from the immense mass of papers placed in his hands a biography perfect in its proportions and in its closely woven texture."

PALL MALL GAZETTE.—"A masterly biography which not only puts into a permanent record Florence Nightingale's whole-souled devotion and humanity, but relates the history of one of the greatest and most fruitful movements of modern time. . . . Sir Edward has written a thousand pages, and never one of them that we could spare."

ATHENÆUM.—"Brilliant, convincing biography. . . . Sir Edward Cook has read his heroine's heart and revealed her secret."

SPECTATOR.—"This book can never be displaced as the authoritative memoir of a great national heroine."

MRS. M. G. FAWCETT IN THE NATION.—"It is impossible to do justice to this delightful book in a single article. It is so full, so varied; it contains such a worthy record of a great character and a long, laborious career of active work that the limits of a review can do no more than call attention to some of its chief features. A mere recital of a few of these should send countless men and women to the book itself."

LONDON: MACMILLAN AND CO., LTD.

BOOKS FOR NURSES

FEEDING AND CARE OF BABY. By F. TRUBY KING, M.B., B.Sc. 8vo. Sewed, 1s. net. Cloth, 2s. net.

NURSING TIMES.—"By the judicious use of many different forms and thicknesses of type it has been possible to compress an enormous amount of information into a page, without in any way producing an overcrowded or too solid appearance. Illustrations abound . . . elucidating the text. Every reader who has to do with babies should at once order a copy of this remarkable monograph."

MEDICAL TIMES.—". . . It contains a wealth of most valuable and practical information on the rearing of infants which cannot fail to be of service to mothers and nurses."

BABIES. A Book for Maternity Nurses. By MARGARET FRENCH, Sister at the General Lying-in Hospital, Lambeth. With Chart and Diagrams. Globe 8vo. 1s. net.

THE HEALTHY BABY. The Care and Feeding of Infants in Sickness and in Health. By ROGER H. DENNETT, M.D. Crown 8vo. 4s. 6d. net.

HOME NURSING. With Notes on the Preservation of Health. By ISABEL MACDONALD, Secretary Royal British Nurses' Association. Globe 8vo. 2s. 6d. net.

A STUDY IN NURSING. By A. L. PRINGLE. Globe 8vo. 1s. net.

MATERIA MEDICA FOR NURSES. By A. S. BLUMGARTEN, M.D. 8vo. 10s. 6d. net.

ANATOMY AND PHYSIOLOGY FOR NURSES. Compiled by DIANA CLIFFORD KIMBER. 8vo. 10s. 6d. net.

CHEMISTRY FOR NURSES. By RUBEN OTTENBERG, M.D. Crown 8vo. 4s. 6d. net.

FOOD FOR THE INVALID AND THE CONVALESCENT. By W. S. GIBBS. Crown 8vo. 3s. 6d. net.

PRIMARY NURSING TECHNIQUE FOR FIRST-YEAR PUPIL NURSES. By ISABEL McISAAC. Crown 8vo. 5s. net.

HYGIENE FOR NURSES. By ISABEL McISAAC. Crown 8vo. 5s. 6d. net.

BACTERIOLOGY FOR NURSES. By ISABEL McISAAC. Crown 8vo. 5s. 6d. net.

SIMPLE LESSONS ON HEALTH FOR THE USE OF THE YOUNG. By SIR MICHAEL FOSTER, K.C.B. Globe 8vo. 1s.

LONDON: MACMILLAN AND CO., LTD.

THE NURSING TIMES

AND

JOURNAL OF MIDWIFERY

WEEKLY ONE PENNY

SOME INTERESTING FEATURES:

Instructive Professional Articles
Massage Articles and News
Illustrated Articles and Notices
The Matron's Page
The Sister's Page
The Head Nurse's Page
The Probationer's Page
Poor Law News (special page)
Free Legal Advice
Free Advice on Charities
Free Advice on Employment
Free Holiday Advice
The fullest Nursing News

AND ALWAYS MANY ADVERTISEMENTS OF VACANT NURSING POSTS

"THE NURSING TIMES" is also invaluable to Midwives
and Maternity Nurses, because, in addition to its full

3

treatment of general nursing matters, it provides *every week* a Supplement entitled

The Journal of Midwifery

This consists of

FOUR SPECIAL PAGES ON MIDWIFERY

which deal fully with the subject from the nurse's point of view, and with the object of helping her practically in her work.

No midwife or maternity nurse who wishes to keep herself well-informed and up-to-date can afford to neglect this weekly journal. There is nothing else published which deals with her special subject in this special way—week by week.

———————

"THE NURSING TIMES" is supplied by all Newsagents and Railway Bookstalls; or can be sent by post direct from the Office at the following rates : 3 months, 1/8 ; 6 months, 3/3 ; 12 months, 6/6.

The addresses of Subscribers can be changed as often as desired.

———————

PREPAID ADVERTISEMENT CHARGES.

Displayed Advertisements, per inch, 6s. Nurses wanted, 21 words, 2s. ; every additional 7 words, 6d.

Training Schools, Nursing and Residential Homes, etc., 21 words, 2s. ; every additional 7 words, 6d.

Nurses disengaged, 21 words, 9d. ; every additional 7 words, 3d.

Advertisements must reach "THE NURSING TIMES" *Offices, St. Martin's Street, London, W.C.,* by 4 P.M. on Wednesday.

Telephone—8830 Gerrard. Telegrams—"Publish, Westrand, London."

THE NURSING TIMES
ST. MARTIN'S STREET, LONDON, W.C.

www.ingramcontent.com/pod-product-compliance
Lightning Source LLC
Chambersburg PA
CBHW081230090426
42738CB00016B/3241